NEW

BASIC

COURSE

IN

PITMAN

SHORTHAND

PITMAN PUBLISHING
CORPORATION

New York
Toronto
London

1.15

Preface

New Basic Course presents the principles of Pitman shorthand in a sequence of sixty short, balanced lessons designed to reduce to a minimum the problems of the learner.

The sixty lessons have been grouped by subject matter in blocks of five. Thus, Lessons 11–15 present the first-place vowels, Lessons 21–25 present the third-place vowels, Lessons 36–40 deal with vowel indication.

Each five lessons is followed by a Mastery Lesson. The purpose of the Mastery Lesson is to provide a review of the principles presented in the lessons preceding it and to provide additional copy for practice. Review charts of short forms and phrases are often included. In certain of the mastery lessons, a challenging type of test letter has been introduced. This letter requires the student to write a line of words that he has been taught in earlier lessons before requiring him to write outlines for three or four new words which employ principles similar to those used in the first line. Here, then, is built-in outline initiation practice developed logically in a simple-to-more-complex pattern.

Abbreviating devices that might appear to the beginning student to be somewhat similar are intentionally separated in the presentation, so that mastery of one may be gained before the other is introduced.

Vowels are included in all outlines through Lesson 36. At that point, the principle of vowel indication is introduced and explained. Teachers will welcome this vowel inclusion as an aid in the teaching of vowel values and placement. From Lesson 37 onward, only certain vowels are shown in the outlines.

In the first ten lessons, all straight copy appears in shorthand. Beginning with Lesson 11, one letter in each lesson appears in type. Phrasing for these letters is indicated by means of raised dots between words, and the total number of words in each letter is given.

Skill in shorthand is most quickly developed by practicing —to the point of automatic response—the shorthand outlines for a basic, high-frequency vocabulary. This accepted premise was the reason for the selection of the 700 Common Words as the teaching medium for the first *Basic Course in Pitman Shorthand*. Over the years, teachers and researchers have reported that an extension of this vocabulary was desirable.

In developing the high-frequency vocabulary introduced in the *New Basic Course*, several lists of the commonest 1,000 words were analyzed. When words appeared on two or more of these lists, they were included in the master list. Natural derivations of root words were then added to the master list to complete it. Students using *New Basic Course* will emerge not only as writers having a satisfactory skill development, but as writers having, in addition, the knowledge of outlines and the power of initiation needed for progressing to higher levels of shorthand skill.

In the writing of the copy, five criteria were employed. First, the bounds were established by the vocabulary presented up to the particular point of theory. Second, emphasis was laid on the words that illustrated the new points of theory being introduced. Third, the subject and content of the sentences had to be as realistic and as businesslike as possible. Fourth, the copy had to have a natural flow so that it would be helpful to the student in reading it and in taking it down. Finally, the copy had to be interesting, because maximum learning is stimulated when the attention level is high.

Because of the restricted vocabulary at the beginning, only sentences are used in the first five lessons. In each lesson, however, the sentences are grouped by subject matter, so that sense extends from one sentence to the next.

In Lesson 6, the first letters are introduced. At this point, the salutations and closes are set in type because of vocabulary limitations, but the bodies of the letters are completely in shorthand. This early introduction of letters in shorthand should prove to be a popular improvement. In lessons thereafter, ten sentences and two letters are included in each lesson.

The principles are stated concisely, and each point is developed with outlines for the related high-frequency words. Each principle is illustrated with a key outline which is set off in a border to highlight it. In some lessons, paragraphs of special information concerning penmanship, phrasing, and speed development have been included.

New Basic Course reflects the suggestions made by hundreds of interested teachers of Pitman shorthand. As experience is gained with this text, it is hoped that teachers will propose additional refinements for future editions.

Table of Contents

LESSON   PAGE

Preface iii

To the Student viii

Introductory Lesson A xii

Introductory Lesson B xv

1. P, B, T, D: Vowels Ā, Ō 2
2. F, V, Th, TH 4
3. K, G, M, N, NG 6
4. Vowels ĕ, ŭ 8
5. L, W, Y 10
  Mastery Lesson 1–5 12
6. PEL Series 14
7. RAY and AR 16
8. Halving of One-Syllable Words . . . 18
9. Halving and Non-Halving 20
10. CH, J, S, Z, SH, ZH 22
  Mastery Lesson 6–10 24
11. VOWELS ă, AH 26
12. Vowels ŏ and AW 28
13. Diphthong Ī 30
14. Diphthong OI 32
15. Medial S-Circle and Medial RAY . . . 34
  Mastery Lesson 11–15 36
16. STEE-Loop 38
17. SEZ-Circle; STER-Loop 40
18. PER Series 42
19. PER and PEL 44
20. Signs for H 46
  Mastery Lesson 16–20 48
21. Vowel Ē 50
22. Vowel ĭ 52
23. Vowels ŌŌ and ŏŏ 54
24. Third-place Vowels and Third Position . . 56
25. Diphthongs U and OW; Triphones . . . 58
  Mastery Lesson 21–25 60
26. N-Hook to Curves 62
27. N-Hook to Straight Strokes 64
28. Double Consonants: Curves 66
29. Reverse Forms 68

30. Intervening Vowels 70
    Mastery Lesson 26–30 72
31. F or V Hook 74
32. Halving Finally Hooked Strokes (I) 76
33. Halving Finally Hooked Strokes (II) 78
34. Circles and Loops to Initially Hooked Strokes . . 80
35. Final Circles and Loops to Finally Hooked Strokes . . 82
    Mastery Lesson 31–35 84
36. Diphones 86
    Vowel Indication 88
37. Vowel Indication: N, F, V, T, and D . . . 90
38. Vowel Indication: Strokes AR and RAY . . . 92
39. Vowel Indication: Upward and Downward L . . 94
40. Vowel Indication: Strokes S and Z 96
    Mastery Lesson 36–40 98
41. Halving for RT, RD, LT, LD 100
42. Halving for MD and ND; Final -TED . . . 102
43. Doubling Curves 104
44. Doubling Straight Strokes 106
45. MP/MB 108
    Mastery Lesson 41–45 110
46. SHUN-Hook to Curves 112
47. SHUN-Hook to Straight Strokes 114
48. Forms for W 116
49. KWAY, GWAY, and WHAY 118
50. SWAY and SEZ Circles 120
    Mastery Lesson 46–50 122
51. Downward L; LER, RER 124
52. Upward SH; SHL, SHR 126
53. Downward and Upward R 128
54. CON (COM) 130
55. Prefixes. 132
    Mastery Lesson 51–55 134
56. Suffixes -ING, -INGS, -MENT, -SHIP . . . 136
57. Suffixes -LY, -ALITY, -ILITY, -ARITY, -ORITY, -WARD . 138
58. Suffixes 140
59. Figures, Units, and Punctuation Marks . . . 142
60. Final Review 144
    Mastery Lesson 56–60 146
    Short Form Chart 148
    Additional Letters 152

To the Student

About Pitman Shorthand

From the day of its conception in 1837, Pitman shorthand has been steadily modified and improved so that today it is fast, accurate, completely reliable, and easy to learn. Office workers and court reporters around the world use it to record a dozen languages. In Pitman shorthand, complete, distinctive outlines are written for all words, long and short. Be proud of the system you are about to study, confident in the knowledge that it is capable of recording the words of even the fastest speakers.

About Learning

You will learn Pitman shorthand faster if you are convinced that you want to learn. Ask yourself why you want to learn shorthand. Sell yourself on the advantage of becoming a really good shorthand writer—better job, higher pay, more satisfaction from your work. Learning to write shorthand is like learning to spell; everyone can learn how if he really wants to—and studies. Your teacher will present all new points of theory and will develop the classroom work to your best advantage. But much of your success in shorthand will depend upon the amount and kind of practice *you* do *at home*. Decide now to do your homework regularly, completely and effectively.

In each theory lesson, listen carefully as your teacher explains the new shorthand principle. Follow exactly the work pattern that is prescribed. When you read the shorthand outlines in the text for the first time, trace each outline with a capped pen as you say the word. When you cannot read an outline immediately, trace it again, thinking through the sounds of the strokes. Then reread the sentences until you can read them smoothly. Good shorthand reading will make you a good shorthand writer. Each extra reading gives you added skill.

Resolve to master every word in every lesson. In the building of your shorthand skill, keep your foundation strong and your skill will stand up at high speeds.

Materials

Use a good quality notebook that is correctly ruled, and use a pen that is flexible and smooth. The notebook should be opened flat on the desk rather than being turned under. This reduces the bulk under your hand (try writing on top of a thick book to get the point) and makes page turning easier.

Posture

Posture is important. A feeling of relaxed alertness can add to the shorthand writer's ability to "take it." Turn your notebook into the best position for you. Rest your forearm on the desk, with your elbow off the edge. Hold your pen firmly but lightly.

Outline Formation

Accurate outline formation depends upon a correct mental picture and upon the care taken in forming outlines. Never at any stage of the study should an outline be *drawn*. At first you may have a tendency to retain the same pressure on the pen throughout the writing of outlines. This lays the foundation for a bad drawing habit, even if the outlines are drawn at reasonable speed. Each outline should be written with a continuous, fluent motion. This kind of writing will not have any detrimental effect on the accuracy of formation—it is merely a necessary speeding up of a basic writing habit. Aim at accuracy of formation, but also always keep in mind the fact that shorthand is intended to be written *quickly*.

Review

Review your theory constantly. It will help you learn to write new outlines correctly, and accurate outline formation is important in the final building of skill. If you write an outline one way today and another way tomorrow, you will hesitate as you decide how to write it on the third day. Make it a point to write outlines only one way—the correct way.

The more outlines you learn, the easier it will become to learn new outlines. There are only a certain number of principles for writing shorthand, and all words are written by these principles. After you have applied a principle to a group of words, you will find that you can apply that principle easily to other words.

It is important, therefore, that you learn the correct outline for each word in every lesson. Then you will apply your shorthand knowledge more correctly and more widely.

Reading

The importance of reading plate shorthand cannot be overemphasized. For a beginning student it is often as beneficial as writing shorthand. When you read plate shorthand you are provided with perfect outlines, outlines that soon become familiar patterns to you. Repeated readings help you form mental images of correct outlines, and correct mental images are the first step in good shorthand writing. Moreover, reading in itself is an important skill needed in transcription. Therefore, read and reread, knowing that every reading adds to your shorthand skill.

Short Forms

The short forms are important cornerstones in building shorthand skill. Since they represent common words, they occur with great frequency when taking dictation. If they are learned thoroughly, the shorthand writer is able to record these words in a minimum of time and so have more time to write longer, less familiar words. The student who does not master the short forms will have great difficulty in taking simple dictation at even the slowest speeds. The secret in achieving this mastery is the right kind of drill—and lots of it.

Develop Speed

To develop shorthand speed, you must develop thinking speed and penmanship speed. *Penmanship speed* refers to the flashing dexterity with which an outline is written once the outline has been formed by the brain. *Thinking speed* refers to the quickness with which the brain can form the correct outline after a word is heard.

Outlines are learned by analysis (the application of theory principles), by association (the building of word families and related words), and by rote memory (the learning of an outline without understanding why it is written as it is). Of these, the surest method is the first. Learning outlines is Step One in writing shorthand.

Outlines are kept fresh in the memory by planned practice and review. It is here that wide reading of shorthand plate material helps most. It is the intermediate step between learning theory and writing automatically. It is Step Two in building writing speed.

At some point in the practicing and reviewing, an outline becomes so well learned that it is written automatically—without time for thinking; this is Step Three. When your teacher says to the class, "Let's try that letter again a little faster," the teacher is using the basic process in building automatic writing—meaningful repetition.

The end product of shorthand skill is not a set of shorthand notes, but an accurate, rapid transcript of dictated material. Transcription that is to be done rapidly and accurately, must be made from shorthand notes that are complete and well written. In shorthand penmanship then, there are two goals: accuracy and speed.

INTRODUCTORY LESSON A

Some of the words on this page appear in their shorthand form instead of in the familiar printed letters. You will be able, without previous instruction in shorthand, ‸ read these words. If for each sign you will supply the word that is needed ‸ complete the sense, you will discover the word that is represented by the shorthand sign.

You will have discovered already, for example, that the word " to " is expressed in shorthand by a small, slanting dash. (The dotted line on which the sign rests represents the ruled line of your notebook.) This small dash is written very lightly in a downward direction so that it rests on the ruled line of your paper.

⋯•⋯ next sign is a heavy dot which also is written on ⋯•⋯ ruled line. You will readily see that this dot expresses ⋯•⋯ word " the."

In this paragraph two additional signs are introduced. One ⋯⋯ them is another small slanting dash.⋅ It is written lightly in a downward direction, but this time it is written above ⋯•⋯ line instead ⋱ on it. This sign, ⋱ course, represents " of." ⋯•⋯ dashes ⋱ and ⋯‸⋯ have ⋯•⋯ same slope, direction, and length; ⋯•⋯ only distinction is in their position. ⋯•⋯ other sign is ⋯⋯ heavy dot that is written above ⋯•⋯ line. When it comes before ⋅ word that begins with ⋅ consonant, this dot represents ⋅ very common word, as in " ⋅ page "; when it comes before ⋯⋯ word that begins with ⋅ vowel, ⋯•⋯ dot represents another very common word, as in " ⋅ apple." No doubt you will have found it ⋅ easy matter ‸ determine that ⋯•⋯ sign ⋅ expresses either " a " or " an."

⋯•⋯ next sign ⋯ₒ⋯ small circle that ⋯ₒ⋯ written on ⋯•⋯ line. It ⋯ₒ⋯ written with ⋯•⋯ same motion that you use in writing ⋯•⋯ longhand letter O; that ⋯ₒ⋯, in ⋯•⋯ direction indicated by this bent arrow ↺ . As you will have discovered, this small circle expresses " is." It ⋯ₒ⋯ also used ‸ express ⋯•⋯ word " his."

xii

...... signs ⌣ two common words that are now introduced are somewhat similar ⌣ appearance. These signs are called strokes. Each ⌣ them ..... shallow curve, written above ...... line. Each stroke ..... written from left ..... right, but ..... stroke ⌣ one word slopes downward, and ..... other stroke ..... written ....
horizontal direction. ...... sign ⌣ expresses "for," and ......
expresses "in." ...... sign ⌣ represents ..... word "any" as well
as "in." ⌣ reading your shorthand notes there ..... never ....
difficulty ⌣ knowing which word ..... required because ..... words
before or after ..... sign .... will always indicate whether it should
be read as "in" or "any."

...... vertical straight stroke, written so that ..... rests on .....
ruled line, ... introduced ⌣ this sentence. Write ..... lightly,
.... downward direction. ..... next sign, ⟨ , ... also written
downwards, but above ..... line, and ..... only half as long as ......
stroke ..... You will observe ⟨ this new sign ..... curved. You
will notice also ⟨ this curve ..... thickened or "shaded." ....
shaded stroke ..... written with just .... slightly heavier pressure on
your pen or pencil. Light strokes like ..... and ⌣ are written
without putting weight on ...... pen; very little more pressure .....
needed ..... write .... shaded stroke.

...... last sign ⌣ this series ..... short .... slanting dash,
written .... upward direction, ... written above ..... line.

...... words which appear .... shorthand ⌣ this lesson occur so
frequently .... all speech .... writing, ... form such .... large
percentage ...... all ..... words used, ⟨ special signs are used ....
them. These special signs are called "Short Forms."

...... writing these short forms, make their length as nearly as
possible ...... same as ...... signs printed ⌣ this text. Observe
carefully .... differences ⌣ length between .... full-length stroke,
.... half-length stroke, ... dash.

xiii

SUMMARY

.... following short forms have been used .... this lesson:
.... to; .... the; .... of; .... a/an; .... is/his; .... for;
.... in/any; .... it; .... that; .... and.

PHRASING

When two or more .... these common words follow each other,
.... signs .... them may often be joined together .... form
shorthand " phrase." .... phrase saves time .... writing, ... thus
increases speed. .... phrase .... formed only when .... easy ....
clear joining can be made. .... signs .... would not join clearly,
.... therefore they are not phrased. Good examples .... phrases
are .... following:

.... of it, ... to it, ... for it, ... in it, ... it is, ... is it,
.... that is, ... is that, ... of that, ... to that, ... for that,
.... in that, ... and that, ... and for, ... and in, ... and is.

(The first sign in a phrase takes its right position with relation to
the line.)

.... form phrases, ... second sign .... provided .... " the."
This sign .... short dash written as shown: ....
.... dash .... " the " .... joined only at .... end
.... another sign; .... never used standing alone, or at .... beginning .... phrase.

In Pitman Shorthand the word *pay* is expressed by the outline ⟍⋮ , a stroke for *p* and a dot for *ay*.

In shorthand writing a word is represented by a combination of signs, just as in longhand a word is spelled with a combination of letters. The signs used in shorthand to express consonants and vowels are much shorter and simpler than the longhand letters, and for this reason shorthand is written much faster than longhand.

Another reason for the speed of shorthand is that in shorthand the *sound* of a word is represented. In longhand the sounds that make up words are spelled in a great variety of ways.

For example, the vowel sound long Ā is spelled in eight different ways in the words *pay*, *they*, *rain*, *reign*, *weigh*, *break*, *same*, *gauge*. In Pitman Shorthand the vowel sound Ā is expressed by the single simple dot shown above. There is a simple sign for each of the sounds heard in English words.

The signs for five consonant sounds and for two vowel sounds are used in these shorthand outlines:

⟍	ape	⟍	pay	⟍	paid
⟍	Abe	⟍	bay	⟍	boat
⎸	ate	⎹	toe	⎸	tape
⎸	aid	⎸	day	⎸	date
⟍	apes	⎸	stay	⟍	soap

NOTE

The consonant strokes ⟍ *p* ⟍ *b* and ⎸ *t* ⎸ *d* are written downwards. They express two pairs of related sounds, a light stroke being used for a light sound and a heavier stroke for the corresponding heavier sound.

The S Circle ...o.... is written with the motion usually used when writing the longhand letter 'O'. It is thus joined on the right side of a straight downstroke: ⅄... *soap*, ↾... *stay*, ⅄₀... *soaps*, ⅄₀... *space*.

When an outline has more than one consonant stroke, the strokes are joined without lifting the pen. The consonant strokes of an outline are written first, and then the vowel sign is placed.

A heavy point or dot, placed close to the middle of a stroke, expresses the long vowel sound $\bar{A}$: ·l... *aid*, ·l·... *day*, ↾·... *stay*.

A heavy dash, placed close to the middle of a stroke, expresses the long vowel sound $\bar{O}$: ⊦⁻... *toe*, ⁻l... *oats*, ⅄... *soap*.

A vowel sign placed on the left side of a stroke is read before the stroke: ·⅄... *ape*, ⁻l... *oat*, ·⅄... *soap*.

A vowel sign placed on the right side of a stroke is read after the stroke: ·⅄... *pay*, ⅄... *boat*, ⅄₀... *space*.

When the vowel sign $\bar{A}$ or $\bar{O}$ comes between two strokes it is placed after the first stroke and read after the first stroke: ⅄... *paid*, ...l·... *date*, ⅄... *boat*.

Two light dashes under an outline indicate a proper name: ...⅄... *Abe*.

The following special punctuation signs are used in shorthand:

Shorthand:	×	⸱P⸱ₓ	!ₓ	=	⟋	{ }
Longhand:	.	?	!	-	—	( )
	Period	Question	Exclamation	Hyphen	Dash	Parenthesis

Other signs are written as in longhand.

NEW

BASIC

COURSE

IN

PITMAN

SHORTHAND

P ⟍ as in pay ⟍	T ⌐ as in tow ⌐
B ⟍ as in bay ⟍	D ⌐ as in day ⌐

Outline Study

S-circle is used to express the sound of S initially and either S or Z finally. It is written as indicated.

ape	⟍ ⟍	Abe	⟍ ⟍	ate	⌐	aid	⌐ ⌐
pay	⟍ ⟍ ⟍	bay	⟍ ⟍	oat	⌐ ⌐	day	⌐ ⌐
soap	⟍ ⟍	boat	⟍ ⟍	tow	⌐ ⌐	date	⌐ ⌐
pace	⟍	base	⟍	stay	⌐ ⌐	space	⟍

Short Forms

Special outlines, called short forms, are written for some common words.

a/an	⋅	I/eye	∨	that	⟨	had/dollar	⌐
the	⋅	you	∩	put	⟍	do	⌐
of	⟍	is/his	○	be	⟍	today	⌐
to	⟍	any/in	⌣	to be	⟍		
and	⟋	for	⟨	it	⌐		

S-circle may be added to short forms: *its* ⌐ *dollars* ⌐

Phrasing

Outlines are often joined. A tick is used for *the* in phrases.

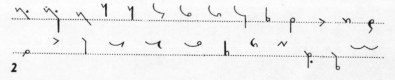

2

Reading and Writing Practice

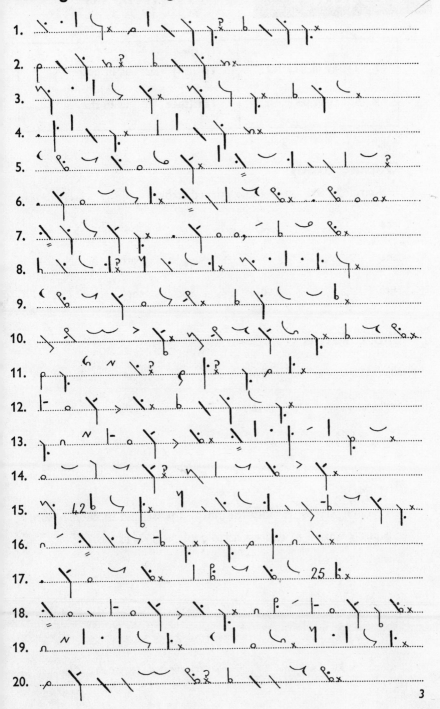

F ⌣ as in face	**Th** (ith) ⌣ as in both
V ⌣ as in save	**TH** (thee) ⌣ as in they

Outline Study

S-circle is written inside a curved stroke.

face	safe	both
fade	save	bathe
faith	vote	they

Short Forms

all	have	them
ought	several	this
we	think	this is

Phrasing

Practice writing rapidly the phrases presented in each lesson.

S-circle is used to express *us* in a phrase: *to us*, *of us*, *for us*

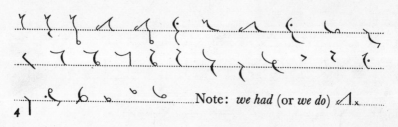

Note: *we had* (or *we do*)

4

Reading and Writing Practice

1. [shorthand outline]
2. [shorthand outline]
3. [shorthand outline]
4. [shorthand outline]
5. [shorthand outline]
6. [shorthand outline]
7. [shorthand outline]
8. [shorthand outline]
9. [shorthand outline]
10. [shorthand outline]
11. [shorthand outline]
12. [shorthand outline]
13. [shorthand outline]
14. [shorthand outline]
15. [shorthand outline]
16. [shorthand outline]
17. [shorthand outline]
18. [shorthand outline]
19. [shorthand outline]
20. [shorthand outline]

5

K ____ as in case ___	M ⌒ as in may ⌒	
G ____ as in gay ___	N ⌄ as in no ⌄	
	NG (ing) ⌄ as in making ⌒⌄	

Outline Study

Read vowel	before stroke ___ ___
	after stroke ___ ___ ⌒ ⌄

S-circle is written on the upper side of K and G.

case	___	same	___	snow	___
sake	___	came	___	make	___
gay	___	game	___	name	___
may	___	no/know	___	take	___

Short Forms

can	___	go	___	thing	___
come	___	him	___	anything	___
give-n	___	himself	___	nothing	___
				something	___

Stroke-NG, for syllable "ing," is added to the following short forms: *being* ___ *doing* ___ *having* ___ *going* ___
In many other words the syllable "ing" is expressed by stroke-NG.

Phrasing

The vowel is always written in *to go* ___, to distinguish the phrase from *to give* ___

In *can you* ___, *give you* ___, *you* is turned.

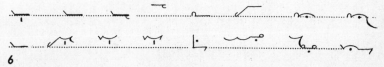

Reading and Writing Practice

1.
2.
3.
4.
5.
6.
7.
8.
9.
10.
11.
12.
13.
14.
15.
16.
17.
18.
19.
20.

7

LESSON 4

VOWELS Ĕ, Ŭ; AND POSITION

Outline Study

(a) The short vowel ĕ is expressed by a light dot placed close to the middle of a consonant stroke.

> beg ⟍

beg ⟍ ⟍ ......   said ...ʃ......   set ...ʃ...ʃ...

debt ...|...|...   sense ...ↄↄ...ↄↄ...   Ted ...|...|...

guess ...ↄ...ↄ...

(b) The short vowel ŭ is expressed by a light dash placed close to the middle of a consonant stroke.

> some ...⌢...

some/sum ...⌢...⌢...   suppose ...⅋...⅋...   up ...⟍...

son/sun ...ↄ...ↄ...   does ...ⱶ...

(c) When an outline begins with a horizontal stroke, it is the first downstroke which rests on the line.

> get ...⌐...

get ...⌐...⌐...   Monday ...⌒|...   Sunday ...⌒|...

enough ...⌒...   month ...⌒...⌒...   unpaid ...⌒|...

                                                 unsafe ...⌒...

Short Forms

as/has ...°...   too/two ...⟍...   manufacture-d ...⌒...

but ...|...   me ...⌒...   on ...|...

who ...⟋...   are ...⟋...   with ...ᴄ...

Phrasing

The dash for *the* is written upward when a sharper angle is thus obtained: *get the* ...⌐... , *set the* ...ʃ...

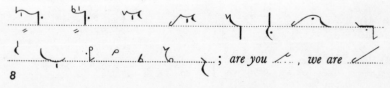

; *are you* ...⟋... , *we are* ...⟋...

8

Reading and Writing Practice

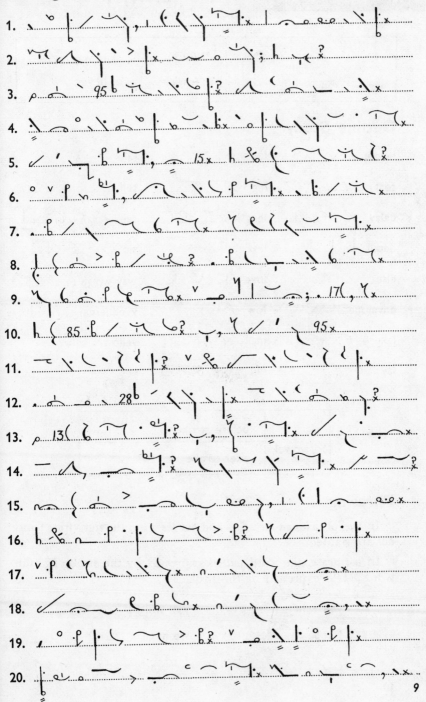

9

L _____ as in less _____	W (way) _____ as in way _____
	Y (yay) _____ as in yes _____

Outline Study

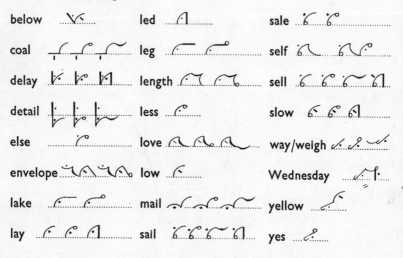

below	led	sale
coal	leg	self
delay	length	sell
detail	less	slow
else	love	way/weigh
envelope	low	Wednesday
lake	mail	yellow
lay	sail	yes

Read vowel	before stroke _____
	after stroke _____

Phrasing

In the phrases *on the* _____ and *but the* _____ the signs for *on* and *but* are slanted.

In a phrase, the word *will* is expressed by the stroke L; the word *hope* is expressed by the stroke P.

you will _____	you will be _____
I hope _____	we hope _____

Reading and Writing Practice

1. [shorthand outlines]

2. [shorthand outlines]

3. [shorthand outlines] 25 [shorthand outlines]

4. [shorthand outlines]

5. [shorthand outlines]

6. [shorthand outlines]

7. [shorthand outlines]

8. [shorthand outlines]

9. [shorthand outlines]

10. [shorthand outlines]

11. [shorthand outlines]

12. [shorthand outlines]

13. [shorthand outlines]

14. [shorthand outlines]

15. [shorthand outlines]

16. [shorthand outlines]

17. [shorthand outlines]

18. [shorthand outlines] 12 [shorthand outlines]

19. [shorthand outlines]

20. [shorthand outlines]

MASTERY LESSON 1-5

Vowels

Read each outline and identify the vowel sounds.

o·	-b	ꝑ	ℯ·
⟋•	ℓ	ℓ	ꞇ⌐·

Write in shorthand, inserting all vowels.

Abe   sells   some   soap   Ted   knows   May   does

S-circle

Write in shorthand.

space   sakes   yes   safes   sense   sales   stays   sons   slows

Outline Mastery

Write in shorthand.

coal   date   enough   get   lake   mail   Monday   month
sale   space   Sunday   unpaid   unsafe   Wednesday   yellow

Short Form Mastery Chart

Practice reading until you can do so without hesitation.

·	`	´	‿	⌣	╱	∘	╲
╷	—	_	╷	╷	v	ℓ	—
—	ℓ	⌢	⌒	∘	╷	∼	⌒
⌣	`	╷	´	╲	℮	∼	⟨
·	⟨	‿	⟨	ℓ	6	╲	╲
╲	⟋	c	╱	∩	⌣	⌣	‿

12

Reading and Writing Practice

1. [shorthand outlines] 31,
2. [shorthand outlines]
3. [shorthand outlines] 750
4. [shorthand outlines] 24
5. [shorthand outlines] 165
6. [shorthand outlines]
7. [shorthand outlines]
8. [shorthand outlines] 35
9. [shorthand outlines] 15?
10. [shorthand outlines] 582
11. [shorthand outlines]
12. [shorthand outlines]
13. [shorthand outlines]
14. [shorthand outlines]
15. [shorthand outlines]
16. [shorthand outlines]
17. [shorthand outlines]
18. [shorthand outlines]
19. [shorthand outlines]
20. [shorthand outlines]

PL (pel) ⎯⎯ as in play ⎯⎯	DL (del) ⎯⎯ as in meddle ⎯⎯
BL (bel) ⎯⎯ as in able ⎯⎯	KL (kel) ⎯⎯ as in close ⎯⎯
TL (tel) ⎯⎯ as in total ⎯⎯	GL (gel) ⎯⎯ as in glow ⎯⎯

Outline Study

The hook for L is written on the same side of a stroke as the S-circle. These double-consonant strokes are called *pel*, *bel*, etc.

The S-circle coming before the double-consonant strokes is written inside the hook.

play ....   meddle ....   club ....

place ....   claim ....   couple ....

able ....   close ....   glow ....

table ....   clothe ....   settle ....

total ....

Short Forms

belief-ve-ved ....   deliver-ed-y ....   people ....

call ....   equal-ly ....   tell ....

till ....

Phrasing

In some phrases, the sign for *I* is shortened.

I may be ....   I believe ....   I can ....   I will ....

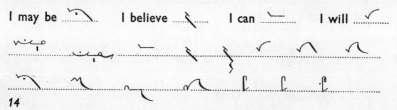

Reading and Writing Practice

A.

Dear Sir: [shorthand] Yours truly,

B.

Dear Mr. Williams: [shorthand] Yours truly,

C.

Dear Tom: [shorthand] Sincerely,

D.

Dear Ted: [shorthand] Sincerely,

Upward **R** (RAY) ...../.....	Downward **R** (AR) .....⌐.....
as in ray ..../....	as in air .....⌐....

Outline Study

(a) When R begins a word, use the upstroke RAY ...../.....

red ...../.....

red/read ...../.....   ray ..../..... .....⌐.....   road ...../.....

railroad ..../.....   race/raise-ing ..../..... .....⌐..... rose .....⌐.....

(b) When R ends a word, use the downstroke AR .....⌐.....

air .....⌐.....

air .....⌐..... .....⌐.....   door ....|-.... ....|-....   fur ....

bear/bare ....   fair/fare ....   pair/pear ....

color ....   force .....   sir ....

dare ....|.... ....|....   four ....   repair ....

Short Forms

hour/our ...../.....   your .....⌐.....   manufacturer .....

regular ...../.....   year .....⌐.....

Phrasing

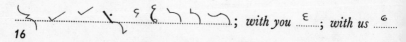

.....; *with you* .....; *with us* .....

16

Reading and Writing Practice

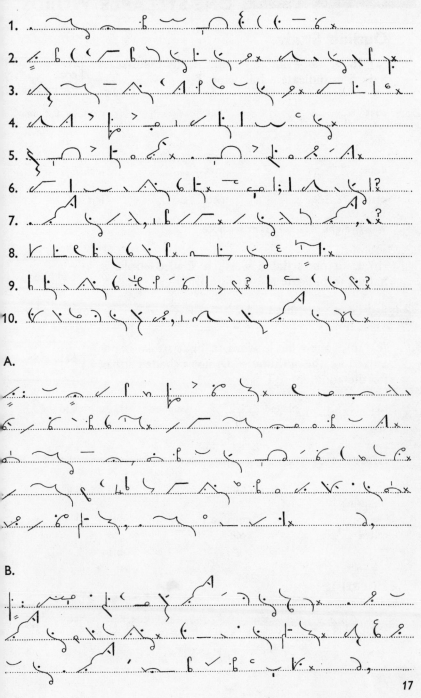

1.

2.

3.

4.

5.

6.

7.

8.

9.

10.

A.

B.

Outline Study

(a) In a one-syllable word, a light stroke is halved to indicate a following T.

coat

coat	wet	cent
cut	yet	late
kept	met	let
plate	net	left
wait/weight	note	

(b) In a one-syllable word, a shaded stroke is halved to indicate a following D.

bed

bed	dead	saved	loved

(c) In a one-syllable word, a light stroke is not halved for the addition of D, nor a shaded stroke for the addition of T.

bet

bet	played	weighed	laid

Short Forms

able to / build-ing	could	gold
called	equaled / cold	told
		oh/owe

Phrasing

; *let us* , *to deliver the*

Reading and Writing Practice

1. [shorthand outline]
2. [shorthand outline]
3. [shorthand outline]
4. [shorthand outline] 15^{75} [shorthand outline]
5. [shorthand outline]
6. [shorthand outline]
7. [shorthand outline]
8. [shorthand outline]
9. [shorthand outline]
10. [shorthand outline]

A.

[shorthand outlines]

B.

[shorthand outlines]

19

Outline Study

(a) In a word of more than one syllable, a stroke is halved to indicate the addition of either T or D.

method

method   relate   settled

doesn't   result   waited

noted   rated

(b) The halving principle is not used when the length of a halved stroke would not clearly show.

effect

effect   select   locate

(c) Half-length RAY is not used unless it is joined to another stroke.

rate

rate   wrote

Short Forms

quite   should   when

sent   special-ly   without

Phrasing

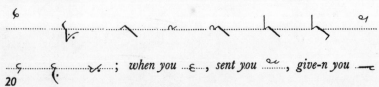

; *when you* , *sent you* , *give-n you*

Reading and Writing Practice

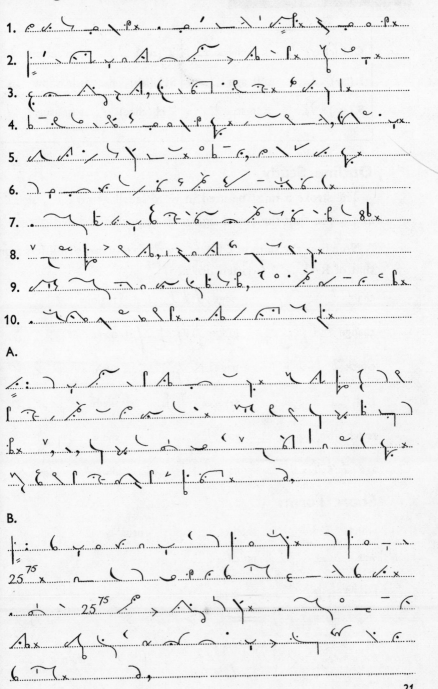

CH (chay)	as in check	**Z** (zee)	as in zealous
J (jay)	as in age	**SH** (ish)	as in show
S (ess)	as in so	**ZH** (zhee)	as in usual*
			* Short form

Outline Study

The stroke S must be used in words such as *say*, *so*, *us*, so that the vowel sign may be accommodated.

Note how the slant of CH (written downward) differs from that of RAY (written upward).

chair

edge

zealous

change

judge

owes

check

page

rush

such

say

shade

touch

so

shape

age

us

show

Short Forms

which

shall

usual-ly

was

much

Phrasing

give-n us

22

Reading and Writing Practice

1.
2.
3.
4.
5.
6.
7.
8.
9.
10.

A.

Dear Joe:

Yours truly,

B.

Dear Chuck:

Yours truly,

23

Halving

WORDS OF ONE SYLLABLE

Light strokes for the addition of **T**.
Heavy strokes for the addition of **D**.
Otherwise halving is not used.

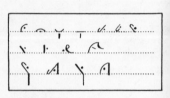

WORDS OF MORE THAN ONE SYLLABLE

For the addition of **T** or **D**.

Outline Mastery

Write these outlines in shorthand, and recall the rule.

| able | enclosing | railroad | repair | kept | left | bed | bet |
| playeds | raising | settled | effect | rate | such | zealous | |

able   enclosing   railroad   repair   kept   left   bed   bet
played   raising   settled   effect   rate   such   zealous

Recognition Practice

Practice reading until you can do so without hesitation.

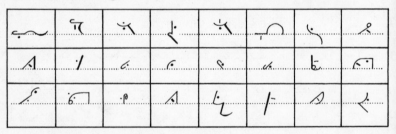

Short Form Mastery Chart

Practice reading until you can do so without hesitation.

Reading and Writing Practice

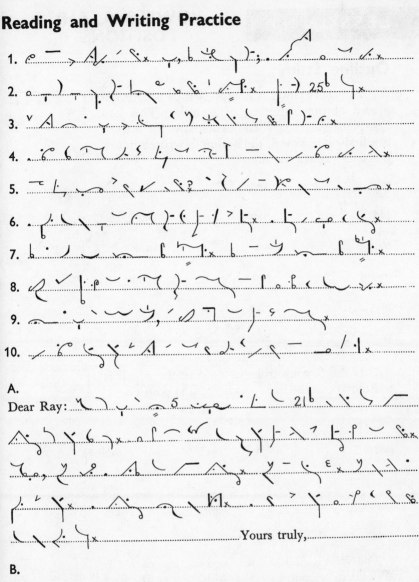

1.

2.

3.

4.

5.

6.

7.

8.

9.

10.

A.

Dear Ray:

Yours truly,

B.

Joe:

When I·was in·your place, you showed me several sets of tables and chairs. As you know, I·have to select several sets for our club building. When I·know all·the details, I·shall·be·able·to judge which sets we ought to·have. Can·you give me all·the details on·the colors you have and your delivery dates? Yours, (64)

(The dots between the words indicate that the outlines are to be joined as phrases.)

VOWELS Ă, AH: POSITIONS

Outline Study

(a) The short vowel Ă is expressed by a light dot placed at the beginning of a stroke. This is a first-place vowel. When the first vowel in a word is a first-place vowel, the outline is written in first position—above the line.

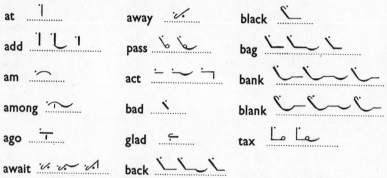

at	away	black
add	pass	bag
am	act	bank
among	bad	blank
ago	glad	tax
await	back	

It is the first upstroke or downstroke which is written above the line to indicate first position.

cash	sample	attach
catch	fact	package

(b) The long vowel AH is a first-place vowel and is expressed by a heavy dot placed at the beginning of a stroke.

Pa   Ma   car   far

The vowels Ā, Ĕ, Ō, Ŭ, used in Lessons 1–10, are called "second-place" vowels. When the first vowel in a word is a second-place vowel, the outline is written in second position—on the line.

Phrasing

26

Reading and Writing Practice

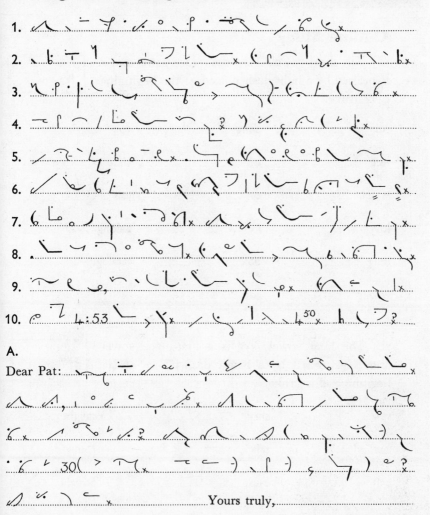

1.
2.
3.
4.
5.
6.
7.
8.
9.
10.

A.

Dear Pat:

Yours truly,

B.

Ted:

You·may know that I·am set to·go away this month for a change of air as a result of·the bad leg which·has kept me in bed of late. I·believe that·such a change may enable me to·come back and face all·the rush that awaits me. I·have checked the safe and·I attach a page that shows the cash, checks, and things you·will·be left with when I go away. The package of tax blanks is·to·be left in·the safe. I·shall·be glad to·have·you stay at Abe's place till I· come back.

Yours,

(*107*)

Outline Study

(a) The short vowel Ŏ is a first-place vowel and is expressed by a light dash placed at the beginning of a stroke.

lot	song	top
not	off	shop
watch	or	job
loss	follow	belong
long	box	catalogue
wrong	got	

(b) The long vowel AW is a first-place vowel and is expressed by a heavy dash placed at the beginning of a stroke.

saw	small	caught
law	talk	thought
ball	cause	bought
tall		

Phrasing

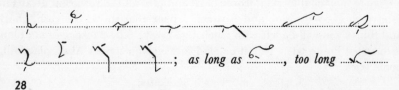

; *as long as* , *too long*

Reading and Writing Practice

1. [shorthand outline]

2. [shorthand outline]

3. [shorthand outline]

4. [shorthand outline]

5. [shorthand outline]

6. [shorthand outline]

7. [shorthand outline]

8. [shorthand outline]

9. [shorthand outline]

10. [shorthand outline]

A.

[shorthand outlines]

B.

Tom:

Do·you think·that it·is too·late in·the game for·us to set up a small shop on·the lot which belongs to Ted Long, close to Abe's place? We·may·have to·take a loss for a month or two, but that·is·not too·long for a thing such·as this. I·believe·the law says that no building can·be set up too close to·the edge of a lot, so·that we·shall·have to·watch this.

Yours,

(85)

Outline Study

(a) The sign ˅ is used for the diphthong sound Ī. It is written in the first vowel place.

> buy/by ˅

buy/by ˅

die

lie

tie

my

nice

sign

side

rise

wise

size

sky

might

fight

light

apply

life

ride

write
right }

mile

smile

alive

time

wide

like

advice
advise }

fire

oblige

(b) The diphthong ˅ can be joined in words such as:

item   night

(c) The first vowel sound always determines the position of the outline.

desire   sometime   supply

reply

Phrasing

Reading and Writing Practice

1. [shorthand outlines]

2. [shorthand outlines]

3. [shorthand outlines]

4. [shorthand outlines]

5. [shorthand outlines]

6. [shorthand outlines]

7. [shorthand outlines]

8. [shorthand outlines]

9. [shorthand outlines]

10. [shorthand outlines]

A.

[shorthand outlines]

B.

To Judge Wise:

We should·be glad to·have·you advise our club on something we·have thought of for a long time   We·have read that·you do sometimes supply aid and advice to clubs like ours when·they write to·you.   Our club building is too small for·us.   We·are obliged to face·the fact that·we·have to·raise enough cash to buy a building of·the right type.   A small club might like to buy ours.   We·shall·be much obliged to·you for your·reply.

Awaiting your advice,   (94)

LESSON 14 — DIPHTHONG OI

Outline Study

(a) The sign ⁊ is used for the diphthong sound OI. It is written in the first vowel place.

boy ˅

boy ˅ ˅   joy ⌐ ⌐ ⌐ ⌐ ⌐   soil ⁊⁶ ⁊⁶

employ ˅ ˅ ˅   voice ⌐ ⌐

(b) The diphthong ⁊ may be joined at the beginning of a stroke.

oil ⌐

Short Forms

January ⌐   never ⌐   knowledge ⌐

February ⌐   November ⌐   myself ⌐

Phrasing

Phrase Mastery Chart

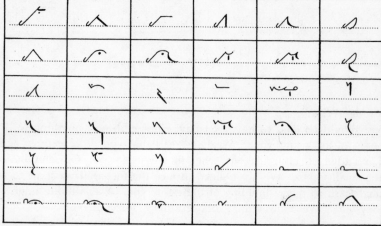

Reading and Writing Practice

1. [shorthand outlines]
2. [shorthand outlines]
3. [shorthand outlines]
4. [shorthand outlines] 12
5. [shorthand outlines]
6. [shorthand outlines]
7. [shorthand outlines]
8. [shorthand outlines]
9. [shorthand outlines]
10. [shorthand outlines]

A.

[shorthand outlines] 12

B.

To a Pair of Wise People:

Do·you like to shop in January? "Yes, who doesn't?" you·reply, "when· you can get a lot for·your cash dollars in·that month." January is·the month of sales in·all·the shops. You·can get all of·the manufacturers' samples in coats and furs, and special buys in boys' clothes. At times, you·may·be·able·to buy something quite unusual. When·you select·the things for·which·you·are going to shop in January, add several days to·the usual time for delivery. Sometimes you·may·have to wait for delivery, but you·can save dollars by waiting.

Yours for January sales, (112)

33

Outline Study

(a) S-circle is written outside of an angle formed by two straight strokes.

| accept |

accept .... desk .... except ....

beside .... custom ....

(b) In the middle of an outline RAY .... is generally used.

| charge |

charge .... March .... per cent ....

fourth .... mark .... Saturday ....

garage .... market .... certain ....

march .... park .... purpose ....

Short Forms

exchange-d .... respect-ed .... yesterday ....

expect-ed .... why ....

Phrasing

Write *much* in full in phrases: *too much* ...., *so much* ....

Reading and Writing Practice

1. [shorthand outlines]

2. [shorthand outlines]

3. [shorthand outlines]

4. [shorthand outlines]

5. [shorthand outlines]

6. [shorthand outlines]

7. [shorthand outlines]

8. [shorthand outlines]

9. [shorthand outlines]

10. [shorthand outlines]

A.

[shorthand outlines]

B.

To·our Customers:

We sell both coal and oil. We should·be glad to·make deliveries to·your garage or shop any day except Sunday. We accept customers who buy a month's or a year's supply at a time. Today's charges are never quite as low as yesterday's. That·is why we advise our customers, when·they can do·so, to·take delivery in March of·the coal and oil for November. We·are·enclosing details of·our charges for supplies delivered to·your place.

Yours,　(86)

Consonants

Upward RAY in the
middle of an outline—

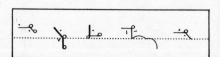

S-circle outside an
angle in the middle
of an outline—

Vowels

First place—

AH	Ă	AW	Ŏ

Diphthongs

First place—

Ī	OI

Position

When the first vowel in a word is a first-place vowel, the outline is written in first position, that is, above the line. When
the first vowel in a word is a second-place vowel, the outline
is written in second position, that is, on the line.

First position
  above the line—

Second position
  on the line—

Outline Mastery

Write these outlines in shorthand

March	package	talking	shop	oblige	employ
market	awaited	thought	long	item	voice

Letters for Dictation

A.

[shorthand content]

B.

[shorthand content]

C.

[shorthand content]

D.

To Some People We Like:

We like certain people for small things, but when·we·have given some thought to·it, the total is never small. We like people who·are alive, who believe that·they can·do things. We enjoy being with people who usually have something· to say, but who say it without too·much talk. We like people who smile, not all·the time, but usually. People we like accept·the fact that all delays are·not on purpose to upset them. They wait when·they have to, without acting like small boys.

-Yours,   (97)

A small loop (called STEE) expresses the sound ST or ZD. It is written half the length of a stroke, in the same direction as the S-circle.

| must |

Outline Study

(a) STEE-loop at the end and in the middle of a word. (Notice how the S-circle is written after the ST-loop.)

must	just	post
lost	best	taste
last	rest	waste
fast	test	August
cost	west	suggest

But notice: *caused* to distinguish it from *cost*.

(b) STEE-loop to add past tense.

based	placed	closed
cased	passed) past)	enclosed
faced		advised
	taxed	

(c) STEE-loop at the beginning of a word.

| state | stop | store |
| step | stock | style |

Short Forms

first   next   most   because

Note the following

special outlines: almost   always   also

Phrases

; *could you*

38

Reading and Writing Practice

1. *[shorthand]*

2. *[shorthand]*

3. *[shorthand]*

4. *[shorthand]*

5. *[shorthand]*

6. *[shorthand]*

7. *[shorthand]*

8. *[shorthand]*

9. *[shorthand]*

10. *[shorthand]*

A.

[shorthand]

B.

To·our Special Charge Customers:

Last August this store put on its first style show for·the sake of·its special charge customers. This first style show lasted four days, just long enough for most people to enjoy it without rushing.

Several customers who saw it at·that time suggested that·we·have a special style show of furs next August. They believe August to·be·the best month for fur sales. Do·you think so?

The enclosed blank, based on·our belief that·the customer knows best, is for·the purpose of·checking·the facts with·you.

Yours for·the best styles at low costs, (*106*)

Outline Study

(a) The sound SES, SEZ, or ZEZ at the end of a word is expressed by a large circle (called SEZ).

masses ⌒

masses ....   faces ....   places ....

causes ....   losses ....   purposes ....

cases ....   passes ....   success ....

(b) The sound STER in the middle or at the end of a word is expressed by a large loop (called STER).

master ⌒

master ....   faster ....   poster ....

(Notice that the SEZ-circle and the STER-loop are also written in the same direction as the S-circle. Final S-circle after SEZ-circle or STER-loop is written as shown.)

Short Forms

influence ....   subject-ed ....   those ....

ourselves ....   themselves ....   would ....

Phrasing

Note the use of the SEZ circle in the phrase: *as soon as* ....

.... ; *would you* ....,

those who ...., *because of* ....

Reading and Writing Practice

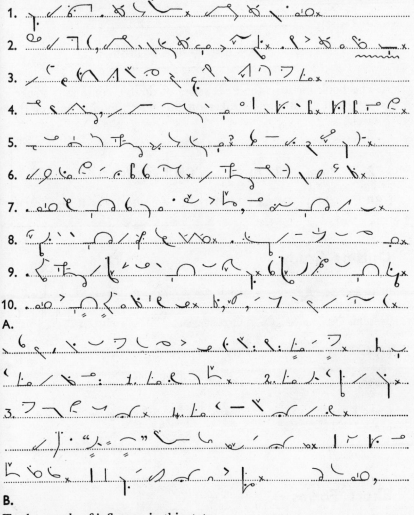

1.
2.
3.
4.
5.
6.
7.
8.
9.
10.

A.

1.
2.
3.

B.

To·the people of influence in·this state:

The people of influence in·any state are those·who vote. You are among them. When·you vote, you·should know something of·the purposes and· the costs of·suggested changes. You·must think of·the effect that delays could·have. A "yes" vote is·not·the best vote in all cases.

We suggest that·the enclosed poster, YOUR VOTE TODAY, be read. It supplies details and gives examples of·the influence of today's votes. It shows several places to cut costs without losses to·the people of·this state. We·believe this knowledge should aid you.

Yours, with faith in·those·who vote, (112)

> ⟍ **PR** (per) as in price

The hook for R in the PER series of double consonant strokes is attached to straight strokes on the side opposite that of the S-circle.

PR ⟍ (per)	**TR** ⌐ (ter)	**CHR** ⌐ (cher)	**KR** ⌐ (ker)
BR ⟍ (ber)	**DR** ⌐ (der)	**JR** ⌐ (jer)	**GR** ⌐ (ger)

Outline Study

price

present

product

paper

brake }
break }

labor

October

try

trust

better

water

dress

address

cry

across

grow

brought

Short Forms

dear ⌐   during ⌐   doctor ⌐   tried ⌐

Phrasing

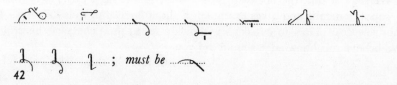

; *must be*

42

Reading and Writing Practice

1. [shorthand outline]

2. [shorthand outline]

3. [shorthand outline]

4. [shorthand outline]

5. [shorthand outline]

6. [shorthand outline]

7. [shorthand outline]

8. [shorthand outline]

9. [shorthand outline]

10. [shorthand outline]

A.

[shorthand outlines]

B.

Dear·Sir:

We·are·enclosing a paper, SUCCESS IN WRITING TODAY, by
DR. PRICE. You·will·note that·you·are to·take a writing test and·that a
close watch on time is·to·be kept. You·must·be·able·to write something
on a given subject in an hour's time. When·you have passed such a test,
we·shall·be·able·to present to·you methods of writing better and faster.

Four of·the most respected names in writing are back of·the methods
we suggest. The papers we·enclose show you examples of·the writings
of all four.

Yours for writing success, *(104)*

43

PER AND PEL

R-hook	L-hook
Side Opposite S-Circle	S-Circle Side
⌒ ⌒ ⌒ ⌐	⌒ ⌒ ⌒ ⌐
pray ⌒	play ⌒

Outline Study

press ⌒ ⌒ ⌒ ⌒   neighbor ⌒ ⌒ ⌒   draw ⌐ ⌐

problem ⌐ ⌐   trouble ⌐ ⌐ ⌐ ⌐   cross ⌐ ⌐ ⌐ ⌐

proper ⌒   drop ⌐ ⌐ ⌐   gray ⌐

bright ⌒ ⌒   dry ⌐ ⌐

Short Forms

large ⌐ ⌐   number-ed ⌒   care ⌐

largely ⌐   great ⌐ ⌐   cared ⌐

larger ⌐   principal-ly/le ⌒   opportunity ⌒

liberty ⌒   trade toward } ⌐ ⌐   particular ⌒

member remember-ed } ⌒   truth ⌐   accord-ing/to ⌐

Phrasing

⌒   ⌒   ⌐   ⌒   ⌒ ; *large number* ⌒

Reading and Writing Practice

1. *[shorthand]*
2. *[shorthand]*
3. *[shorthand]*
4. *[shorthand]*
5. *[shorthand]*
6. *[shorthand]*
7. *[shorthand]*
8. *[shorthand]*
9. *[shorthand]*
10. *[shorthand]*

A.

[shorthand]

B.

Dear Neighbors:

I suggest that·we take this opportunity to press our case for proper lights. We should·have brighter lights and a larger number of·them. The truth is·that it·is·not safe to cross our roads at night. We all remember·the trouble last October and·the particular problems we faced. Let·us not drop our case this time. Let·us take great care to present it in·the proper way.

Yours, (75)

H ⌒ (upward HAY) as in hope ⌒	H ⁄ (tick-H) as in home ⌒
H ⌐ (downward HAY) as in high ⌐	H (dot-H) as in perhaps ⟍

Outline Study

(a) Upward HAY is generally used.

hope ⌒ ⌒ ⌒ ⌒   hat ⌐ ⌐   height ⌐

hang ⌒   hot ⌐   hotel ⌐

head ⌐ ⌐ ⌐ ⌐

(b) Downward HAY is used:

    (1) When H is the only consonant sound.

    (2) In words beginning with "high."

    (3) Before K and G.

hay ⌐   high ⌐ ⌐   hog ⌐ ⌐

(c) Tick-H is used before M, L, and R.

home ⌒ ⌒   hold ⌐ ⌐ ⌐   horse ⌐ ⌐ ⌐

hall ⌐ ⌐   health ⌐   her ⌐

help ⌐ ⌐ ⌐ ⌐   hair ⌐   heart ⌐ ⌐ ⌐

hole ⎫
whole ⎭ ⌐ ⌐

(d) In a few cases H may be expressed by a dot.

perhaps ⟍

Phrasing

all right ⌐

46

Reading and Writing Practice

1. [shorthand outlines]

2. [shorthand outlines]

3. [shorthand outlines]

4. [shorthand outlines]

5. [shorthand outlines]

6. [shorthand outlines]

7. [shorthand outlines]

8. [shorthand outlines]

9. [shorthand outlines]

10. [shorthand outlines]

A.

[shorthand outlines]

[shorthand outlines]

[shorthand outlines]

[shorthand outlines] 12 [shorthand outlines] 13 [shorthand outlines]

[shorthand outlines]

B.

Dear Dr. Hall:

We·are·glad to know that·you·will·be with·us sometime in August. We·shall·have lots of space for·you and your club, and we·shall·be·able·to take care of·you in a proper way. You·will·have several hot days during your stay, but our place is high enough so·that it·should·be quite all·right for riding.

Let me know in a couple of days the number of·people who·will come. We always like to·have your club with·us.

Yours,   (*92*)

Consonants

HAY: Upward, generally used

Downward, when standing alone
or before K and G

Tick, initially before M, L, R

Dot, medially in long outlines

R-hook

L-hook

SEZ-circle

STEE-loop

STER-loop

Outline Mastery

Write these outlines in shorthand:

stopped   best   testing   hold   losses   problem   high

store   west   suggesting   hope   masters   trouble   perhaps

etters for Dictation

A.

[shorthand outlines]

B.

[shorthand outlines]

C.

(a) *[shorthand outlines]*

(b) *[shorthand outlines]*

(c) *[shorthand outlines]*

D.

To those·who like to·take tests:

Write across the page:

applies   ball   like   weighed   sales   far   price   toy   less   past   red   across

Below, write:

place	boil	lake	wide	soils	fire	press	tie	loss	post	ride	cross
apples	bell	lack	wade	sells	fare	prize	tow	laws	paced	road	cries
applause	bale	luck	wad	souls	four	praise	toe	lies	paused	rod	acres

Check your results. Can·you tell why this test is suggested at·this time?

Yours for success,   (*78*)

49

Outline Study

(a) The long vowel Ē is expressed by a heavy dot written close to the end of a stroke. Ē is called a third-place vowel. When the first vowel in a word is a third-place vowel, the outline is written in the third position, that is, the first upstroke or downstroke is written half-way through the line.

each

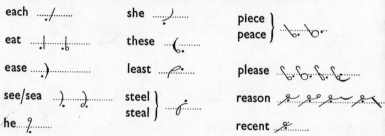

each ...../......   she ....../......   piece } peace }

eat ....|..|.....   these ...(......

ease ....)......   least ...ρ....   please

see/sea)..)..   steel } steal }   reason

he ?......   recent

(b) When a third-place vowel comes between two strokes, the sign is written in front of the second stroke.

teach ....|....

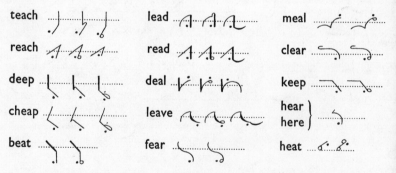

teach   lead   meal

reach   read   clear

deep   deal   keep

cheap   leave   hear } here }

beat   fear   heat

(c) Position is determined by the first vowel.

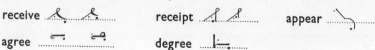

receive   receipt   appear

agree   degree

Phrasing

50

Reading and Writing Practice

[shorthand outlines, items 1–10 and a letter in shorthand]

To all who apply to·us for jobs:

When·you apply for·your first job with·us, you·receive·the enclosed test. We·believe·that you·should·be·able·to say *yes* to each of·these items:

1. Can·you talk to most people with ease and without fear?
2. Do·you·like to know·the reasons back of·the things you have to·do?
3. Are·you at sea at times, when·the results are·not quite clear to·you?
4. Are·you able·to change methods that must·be changed, without waste of·time?
5. Are·you able·to keep on checking details with care?

Yours for·the job you·can do best, (110)

51

Outline Study

(a) The short vowel Ĭ is expressed by a light dot written close to the end of a stroke. Ĭ is a third-place vowel. When it comes first in a word, the outline is written in third position, that is, the first upstroke or downstroke is written half-way through the line.

city

city   sit   invoice

if   list   inch

ill   still   simple

(b) When a third-place vowel comes between two strokes, the sign is written in front of the second stroke.

bill

bill   figure   pretty

big   limit   ring

bridge   hill   ship

bring   live   trip

business   mill   visit

drink   pick   similar

(c) The first-sounded vowel in a word determines its position.

capital   promise   service

office   credit   notice

hesitate   April   benefit

satisfy

Phrasing

   ; *in this city*   , *on us*   ,

each year

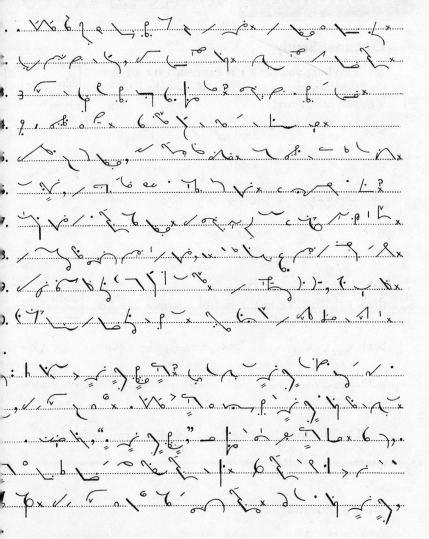

Why do·you enjoy visits to big cities?

Is·it that a visit to any of·the bigger cities brings you living as you like best? Is·it that·you enjoy going to·the big ball games, the races, fightings, night clubs, parties, and plays in·the city?

Do·you·like to·be·able·to sit still and·watch any TV show you select ithout being limited in·any·way? Do·you like·the closeness, size, and yle of·the buildings in·the city?

Why not visit our city next?

Yours for·the joys of·city living, (99)

Outline Study

(a) The long vowel OO is expressed by a heavy dash written close to the end of a stroke. OO is a third-place vowel.

blue

blue   cool   lose

shoe   food   move

use   group   poor

true   July

(b) The short vowel OO is expressed by a light dash written close to the end of a stroke. OO is a third-place vowel.

book

book   look   pull

took   fully   wood

(c) The first-sounded vowel in a word determines its position.

assure   into

Short Forms

different-ce   wish   insurance

what

Phrasing

In phrases, *would* may be expressed by   :

; *Yours truly*

54

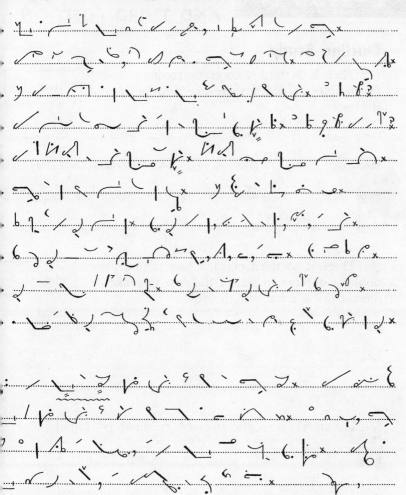

ar·Sir:

Success in group living is based on several things. Not·the least of·these
the problem of *who* does *what*. In·this group, we all take·the jobs we·
nk we·can·do best. This method assures simple living.

For example, two of·us enjoy doing·the marketing. Two like to set·the
les and to clear up. I pick up and deliver·the mail and·the papers.
e bigger boys take charge of·the moving.

Some people like it. No booklet can tell·you why. You have to live
o know.

Yours·truly,   (*98*)

THIRD-PLACE VOWELS AND THIRD POSITION

Outline Study

(a) There is no third position (use second position) for outlines in which there are only horizontal strokes.

	seen .ei.

seen .ei.	seem .om. .om. .ei.	good .y.
soon .oi.	miss .em. .em. .em.	increase .ei. .ei. .em.
since .eie.	meet .em. .em. .em.	include .ei. .ei. .ei.
single .ei.	six .ei. .ei. .ei.	cook .y. .y.

(b) There is no third position (use second position) for outlines in which the first upstroke or downstroke is a half-length stroke.

	did ..l..

did ..l..	system .e. .e.	written .en.
foot .ei. .ei.	east ..l.	indeed .ei.
sheet ../.	little .ei.	needed .ei.

(c) The vowel *i* is used to represent the final "*y*" sound.

happy .ei. .ei. .ei.	heavy .ei. .ei.	badly .er.
family .ei. .ei.	daily .er. .er.	thoroughly .ei.
party .ei. .ei.	lately .ei.	money .em. .em.
copy .en. .en. .en.	lady .ei. .ei.	many .em.
authority .ei. .ei.	baby .er. .er.	likely .er.

Phrasing

.ei. .ei. ; *by all* .em. ; *at all* .l.

Reading and Writing Practice

1. [shorthand outlines]

2. [shorthand outlines]

3. [shorthand outlines]

4. [shorthand outlines]

5. [shorthand outlines]

6. [shorthand outlines]

7. [shorthand outlines]

8. [shorthand outlines]

9. [shorthand outlines]

10. [shorthand outlines]

A.

[shorthand outlines]

B.

Dear Sir:

Having too·little money is indeed a big problem. It·seems bigger when· the little bills are still unpaid. It·is biggest when·you are·not able·to meet· the big bills on time. Maybe your credit system is all wrong for·your family's capital. If·this·is true, a single visit should supply all·the details that are needed for a better system.

Our little booklet, YOUR FAMILY'S CAPITAL AND CREDIT, includes several wise ways of making your money do a better job for·you. Many people have used the advice given in·this booklet with good results.

Yours·truly, (*103*)

Outline Study

(a) The sign …n… is used to express the diphthong sound Ū. It is a third-place sign, but it is sometimes joined to a preceding stroke.

duty

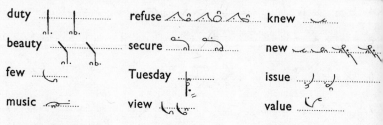

duty   refuse   knew

beauty   secure   new

few   Tuesday   issue

music   view   value

presume   due

Note how …n… is turned for convenience in words like …

(b) The sign …∧… is used to express the diphthong sound OW. It is also a third-place sign, but it is sometimes joined. Strokes with a joined diphthong at the end may be halved for either *T* or *D*.

out

out   cloud   south

allow   crowd   about

announce   mouth   doubt

Note the special outline for *now* …∧…   house

(c) A small dash is added to any diphthong sign to express a following vowel. This combination is called a triphone.

buyer

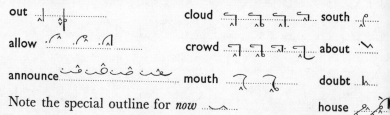

buyer   power   valuable   employee

Short Forms

beyond   how   itself

Phrasing

; *how much*

We·presume that·you enjoy good music. Have·you sometimes wished at·you knew how to secure·the benefits of·the best in music for·your mily? Beyond doubt, you would like your family to know about·the auty and power of music you wish them to remember.

Why not have us mail you a copy of MUSIC TO ENJOY? In·this sue we announce a new book of·such value that each house should·have copy. Please allow us to tell·you how you·can secure this book and how. uch you·will enjoy it.

                                   Yours·truly,   (*101*)

Vowels

Third place

Ē	Ĭ	ŌŌ	ŎŎ
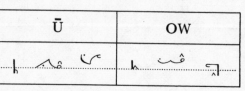

Diphthongs

Third place

Ū	OW

(notice how diphthongs are sometimes joined to strokes)

Triphones

Represent a vowel sound
added to a diphthong

Third Position

Outline written half-way *through* the line
when the first consonant is a downstroke
or an upstroke.

Outline written *on* the line
1. When the first consonant is a half-
length downstroke or upstroke.

2. When the outline contains only
horizontal strokes.

Short Form Mastery

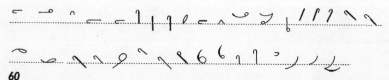

Letters for Dictation

A.

(shorthand outline)

B.

(shorthand outline)

C.

(shorthand outline)

D.

To those·who like to·take tests:

Write across·the page:

beauty   caught   least   allowed   mail   night   appear   raises   saw   sin   steal

Below, write:

beat	cat	last	lady	meal	net	pair	races	say	sign	still
bet	coat	list	lead	mile	not	poor	rises	see	son	style
bit	cut	lost	led	mill	note	power	roses	so	seen	stale
bought	cot	laced	load	mule	neat	pour	ruses	sigh	soon	stole

Yours for good results, (72)

61

Outline Study

(a) A small hook at the end of a curve adds N.

> then ......

then	man	often ......
even	men	seven ......
fun	mean	shown ......
fine	nine	than ......
known		thin ......

(b) S-circle is added by writing the circle inside the N-hook.

> lines ......

lines	machines	phones ......
loans	mines	

Short Forms

opinion ......   own ......   within ......

Phrasing

Reading and Writing Practice

1. *[shorthand outlines]*

2. *[shorthand outlines]*

3. *[shorthand outlines]*

4. *[shorthand outlines]*

5. *[shorthand outlines]*

6. *[shorthand outlines]*

7. *[shorthand outlines]*

8. *[shorthand outlines]*

9. *[shorthand outlines]*

10. *[shorthand outlines]*

A.

[shorthand outlines]

B.

Dear·Sir:

We·are announcing a new and simpler loan service system today. A man that owns his own business may apply for a loan at any of·our nine city offices any day or evening, even by phone. Often a man has bills at home that·must·be paid. In·such·cases, it·can·be shown that·it·is much better not to·draw on capital.

The right thing to·do is to phone us for a loan. You·will not have to pay back·the loan within any certain time. You·can then pay your bills and keep your capital for business use.

Yours·truly,   (*107*)

63

LESSON 27

N-HOOK TO STRAIGHT STROKES

A small hook at the end of a straight stroke, written on the opposite side to the S-circle, adds N.

again ⌐

Outline Study

(a)

again ⌐	American ⌐	obtain
plan	gone ⌐	join
ran	happen	anyone

(b)

begin	pain	sudden
between	plain / plane	one / won
engine	taken	broken
chain	upon	open
train	hundred	done
gain		

(c)

skin	bulletin	brown
win	June	green
clean	down	

Short Forms

been \   general-ly /   organize-d

Phrasing

The N-hook is also used to express *been*, *than*, and *own*, i phrases.

been: ⌐   ; than: ; own:

64

Reading and Writing Practice

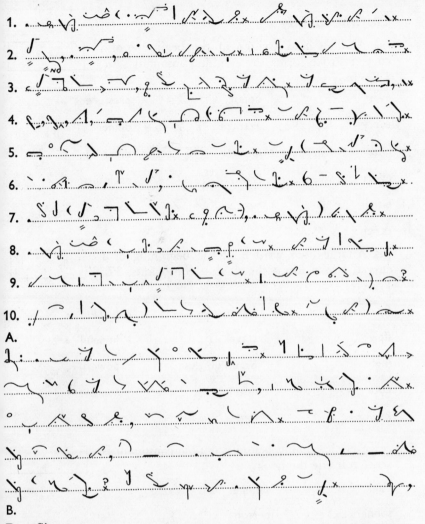

1.

2.

3.

4.

5.

6.

7.

8.

9.

10.

A.

B.

Dear·Sir:

We·are planning to open one of·our·own dry cleaning stores in Brown
Road on June 12. We·have·been in just one business—Masters Dry Cleaning Service—for many years. This·is·the one line of business we·know how
to·run. The present chain of·Masters Dry Cleaning Service stores has
taken a long·time to plan, build, and run.

Today the American people expect fast, thorough, organized, and pleasing
service at reasonable prices. Masters' picks up and delivers in one day
when·this service is needed.

Yours·truly,   (94)

DOUBLE CONSONANTS: CURVES

Outline Study

(a) A small hook written at the beginning of a curved stroke forms the double consonants, *FR*, *VR*, etc.

> ever ⟨shorthand⟩

ever	honor	pressure
every	average	dinner
offer	manner	differ
effort	Friday	enclosure
either	measure	favor
other		

(b) A large hook written at the beginning of a curved stroke forms the double consonants, *FL*, *VL*, etc.

> fly ⟨shorthand⟩

fly	flown	helpful
flew	travel	hopeful
flight	beautiful	powerful
floor	develop	approval
flower	final	

(c) S-circle coming before a double consonant is written inside the hook.

> safer ⟨shorthand⟩

safer	summer
sooner	personal

Short Forms

mere	young	pleasure
Mr.	younger	advertise-d-ment
near	youngest	govern-ed
thank-ed	over	government
owner	however	respectful-ly

66

Reading and Writing Practice

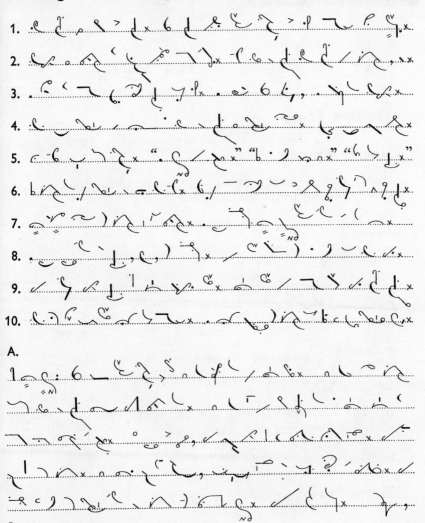

1.

2.

3.

4.

5.

6.

7.

8.

9.

10.

A.

B.

Dear Mr. Manners:

Thank·you for your·reply to·our advertisement. First, let me say that· we·do teach flying and·that we·do have government approval.

The average young person can fly. However, it takes a little effort to master. Flying, in some ways, is safer than other means of·travel. It differs in that·it offers beautiful views and greater pleasure. Why not come on a flight with·us this Friday? When·you have flown, take time to·think it over. Then give·us your final thought. We·are hopeful you·will join us.

Yours truly, (*98*)

FR ⌐ as in free ⌐	ThR) as in three)
VR ⌐ as in river ⌐	THR) as in weather ⌐

Outline Study

(a) FR, VR, ThR, and THR have additional or "reverse" forms as shown above.

(b) The reverse form is used in a one-stroke word which does not begin with a vowel.

through ⌐

through
threw }))

three ⌐

free ⌐

freight ⌐

(c) The reverse form is used to obtain convenient joinings, as after a left-to-right stroke.

cover ⌐

cover ⌐ ⌐

discover ⌐ ⌐ ⌐

brother ⌐ ⌐ ⌐

gather ⌐ ⌐ ⌐

river ⌐ ⌐

silver ⌐

weather ⌐

fresh ⌐

(d) The FL and VL hook also is reversed to obtain a more convenient joining.

reflect ⌐

reflect ⌐

rival ⌐

novel ⌐

Short Forms

from ⌐   their
             there })   third)   very ⌐

Phrasing

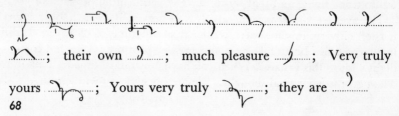

; their own) ; much pleasure) ; Very truly

yours ⌐ ; Yours very truly ⌐ ; they are)

Reading and Writing Practice

1. [shorthand outlines]
2. [shorthand outlines]
3. [shorthand outlines]
4. [shorthand outlines]
5. [shorthand outlines]
6. [shorthand outlines]
7. [shorthand outlines]
8. [shorthand outlines]
9. [shorthand outlines]
10. [shorthand outlines]

A.

[shorthand outlines]

B.

Dear Mr. Knight:

This·is to tell·you that beginning Friday, June 3, there·will·be an increase in freight rates on·the Green River Railroad System. This long overdue rise in freight rates has finally received·the approval of·the·government's Rate Authority. It·is·the third time in two·years that·we·have·had to apply for higher freight rates to cover rising costs.

We·can assure·you that·there·will·be no change in·the effort to·give·you· the very best service at·all times. The added charge of a few cents on each package accepted by·us for delivery should help.

Yours·very·truly, (*109*)

Outline Study

Sometimes, to obtain shorter outlines, the hooked sign is used even though a vowel other than ĕ comes between the double consonant. The vowel is expressed as follows:

(a) A dot vowel sound, by writing a small circle in place of the dot.

regard

regard ....   dark ....   But notice:

But notice: regret ....   direct ....   girl ....

children ....   engineer ....   thirty ....

garden ....   term ....

(b) A dash vowel sound, by writing a dash through the double consonant.

before

before ....   corner ....   purchase ....

church ....   court ....   record ....

college ....   forget ....   Thursday ....

coarse / course ....   north ....

Short Forms

character ....   more ....   remark-ed ....

characteristic ....   nor / in our ....   remarkable-y ....

Phrasing

In the middle or at the end of a phrase, *he* is written as a heavy tick .ı.x. .... But notice: ....

any more .... ; *more than* .... ; *never been* ....

70

Reading and Writing Practice

1. [shorthand outline]
2. [shorthand outline]
3. [shorthand outline]
4. [shorthand outline]
5. [shorthand outline]
6. [shorthand outline]
7. [shorthand outline]
8. [shorthand outline]
9. [shorthand outline]
10. [shorthand outline]

A.

[shorthand outlines]

B.

Dear Miss Brown:

We·regret very·much that·we·are·not able·to add any·more names to· our list of·employees in training in·our College Corner Shop. We gather from·your recent note that·you have not·been employed before. Did you forget to·read·the bulletin regarding·the training course in·our College Corner Shop? Three·years of·college and three summers as a paid employee are needed before your name can·be listed.

We·are·pleased with your remark that·the items you purchased for·your freshman year have given·you so·much pleasure. These items are again in· favor. Yours·truly, *(106)*

Read and write the following

Consonants

N-hook to curves

N-hook to straight strokes

R-hook to curved strokes

L-hook to curved strokes

FR, VR, ThR, THR—
Reverse forms used in one-syllable words

When joining is more convenient

Vowels

Intervening vowels between double consonants:

Dot-vowel sounds

Dash-vowel sounds

Outline Mastery

Write these outlines in shorthand.

then	fly	rival	again	effort	either	personal
than	flew	novel	sudden	freight	through	forget

Letters for Dictation

A.

[shorthand outlines]

B.

[shorthand outlines]

C.

[shorthand outlines]

D.

Dear Miss Record:

Are·you ready to·take Test Three today? Take a wide sheet of paper with lines. Write·the first line across·the page. Then write·the related outlines in list form on·the lines below.

better	copy	down	flew	height	home	join	pull	pain	shown	tan	voice
butter	cap	dine	fly	hat	ham	John	pile	open	shine	tone	vise
bitter	keep	done	flaw	hot	hem	June	pale	pine	sheen	ton	views
batter	cope	dawn	flow	hate	hum	Jane	Paul	pen	shun	town	vase
beater	occupy	dean	flee	heat	whom	Jean	appeal	pin	ocean	tune	vows

Yours for still better marks, (*103*)

F OR V HOOK

(a) A small hook at the end of a straight stroke, written on the same side as S-circle, adds either F or V.

above ⌐

above ⌐   gave ⌐   serve

chief   proof/prove   wave

drive   relative   wife

half

Notice that a final S-circle is written inside the F or V hook.

(b) The F or V hook may be used in the middle of a word.

advance ⌐

advance   provide

perfect   refer

profit   driving

(c) There is no F or V hook to curves. The small hook at the end of a curve expresses N.

five ⌐

five   knife   move

Short Forms

advantage   difficult   represent-ed

behalf   difficulty   representative

Phrases

F or V hook is used in phrases to add *of* or *have*.

of: ; have:

74

Reading and Writing Practice

1. [shorthand outline]
2. [shorthand outline]
3. [shorthand outline]
4. [shorthand outline]
5. [shorthand outline]
6. [shorthand outline]
7. [shorthand outline]
8. [shorthand outline]
9. [shorthand outline]
10. [shorthand outline]

A.

[shorthand outlines]

B.

Dear Mr. House:

How·long has·it been since you have taken a pleasure trip? Has·it been one year, or more? Even if·you had a fine trip just last·year, it·should· not·be too difficult for·you and your wife to select one today from·the enclosed travel booklet. Our travel representative is very happy to serve you in every way he·can. You·should·not hesitate to call upon him for help to plan a perfect trip. His services are there in a number·of ways for· your use and pleasure.

Yours·truly, (*109*)

HALVING FINALLY HOOKED STROKES (I)

A straight stroke that is hooked for N is halved to indicate a following T or D.

paint	⟍
pound	⟍

(a)

paint	point	extent
count	print	instant
account	spent	apparent
discount	want	president
grant	went	
plant	won't	

(b)

pound	ground	depend
planned	round	turned
spend	second	learned
extend	stand	behind
bind	wind	
kind	trained	

Short Forms

cannot	gentleman	gentlemen

Phrases

Reading and Writing Practice

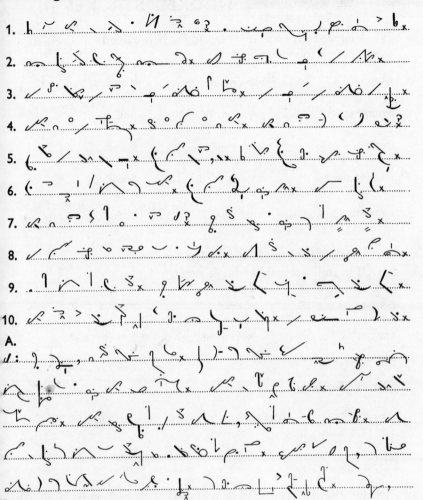

1.

2.

3.

4.

5.

6.

7.

8.

9.

10.

A.

B.

Gentlemen:

I·was very glad to·receive a copy of·your bound booklet, "Unusual Ground Planting." This booklet seems·to·be just what we·have wanted for a long·time for use in·the Garden Club. Is there any discount for hundred-lot purchases? Do·you have any other booklets of about·the same size on similar subjects? We·would like to·learn much more about such things as wind, weather, and·water, and·their effects upon planting. Please mail me·the printed sheet needed for opening a special account with·you, and a list of·your other booklets.

Yours·truly,   (103)

(a) A curved stroke that is hooked for N is halved to indicate a following T or D.

amount ⟨shorthand⟩

amount ⟨shorthand⟩   movement ⟨shorthand⟩   demand ⟨shorthand⟩

event ⟨shorthand⟩   payment ⟨shorthand⟩   find ⟨shorthand⟩

front ⟨shorthand⟩   settlement ⟨shorthand⟩   found ⟨shorthand⟩

development ⟨shorthand⟩   statement ⟨shorthand⟩   friend ⟨shorthand⟩

moment ⟨shorthand⟩   mind ⟨shorthand⟩   land ⟨shorthand⟩

(b) A straight stroke that is hooked for F or V is halved to indicate a following T or D.

gift ⟨shorthand⟩

gift ⟨shorthand⟩   halved ⟨shorthand⟩   proved ⟨shorthand⟩

draft ⟨shorthand⟩   approved ⟨shorthand⟩   served ⟨shorthand⟩

Short Forms

though ⟨shorthand⟩   although ⟨shorthand⟩   appointment ⟨shorthand⟩

Phrases

In phrases, the word *not* is represented by the addition of N-hook to a halved stroke: thus, *do not* ⟨shorthand⟩, *had not* ⟨shorthand⟩, *did not* ⟨shorthand⟩, *you are not* ⟨shorthand⟩, *I am not* ⟨shorthand⟩, *I will not* ⟨shorthand⟩, *it will not be* ⟨shorthand⟩

Correcting Notes

If you write an incorrect outline, circle it, and write the correct outline.

78

Reading and Writing Practice

1. [shorthand]
2. [shorthand]
3. [shorthand]
4. [shorthand]
5. [shorthand]
6. [shorthand]
7. [shorthand]
8. [shorthand]
9. [shorthand]
10. [shorthand]

A.

[shorthand]

B.

Gentlemen:

We·have a young friend who·has a very unusual gift for pleasing dependent people, even those most difficult to·please. We know this because we·have never found her equal in·time of·trouble. Other families in·this development apparently have discovered·the same thing, because·the demand for·her help grows with every passing moment. She has a very·good mind, a pleasing personality, and·the kind·of fine character we·are bound to·respect and honor. We·have·just found out that she would like to teach, but I· do·not think she is yet a citizen. Could·you suggest a plan for·her?

Very·truly·yours,   (109)

CIRCLES AND LOOPS TO INITIALLY HOOKED STROKES

At the beginning of an outline, when a circle or loop comes before a *straight* double-consonant stroke of the .... *per* series, it is written on the R hook side of the sign. The circle or loop thus includes the R.

strong	⌐
stouter	↓

(a)

strong ....   spring ....   stream ....

separate ....   straight ....   street ....

spread ....   strange ....   stouter ....

(b) In the middle of an outline, both the S-circle and the hook of a double-consonant stroke are shown.

extra	....
possible	....

extra ....   express ....   possible ....

destroy ....   industry ....   explain ....

distribute ....

(c) Notice how medial S is written in the following outlines.

describe ....   disagree ....

Short Forms

spirit ....   surprise ....   description ....

Paragraphs

In your shorthand notes, indicate the start of a new paragraph by indenting or by writing the sign .... //

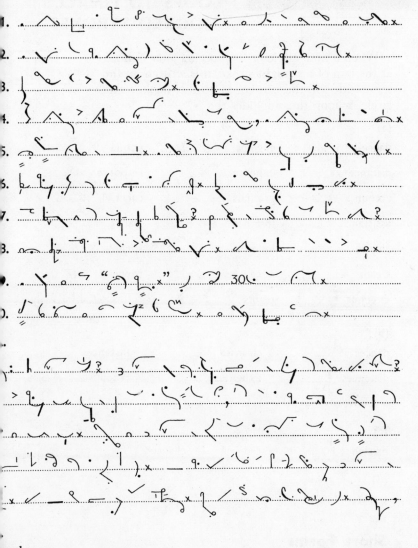

I·have·been looking through·the Spring catalogue you sent to·me, and· there·are a number· of items that I·want. Do·you suppose that I·can have delivery of all items within one·month? If·not, perhaps you·will want to separate those items that can·be delivered at·this·time from those that· will·be delayed. I·am enclosing with·this note the list of items I·want, and·I·hope·that it·will·not·be too·long before I receive them.

Very·truly·yours,   (*89*)

FINAL CIRCLES AND LOOPS TO FINALLY HOOKED STROKES

When a final circle or loop occurs after N-hook at the end of a straight stroke, it is written on the same side of the stroke as the N-hook. The circle or loop thus includes the N.

dance

(a)

dance	engines	points
distance	expense	response
accounts	grounds	turns
assistance	instance	learns
chance	kinds	spends
cleans	once	towns
depends	plants	trains
		wants

(b)

dances	cleanses	instances
distances	expenses	responses
chances		

(c)

danced   distanced   chanced   against

(d)

spinster

Short Forms

balance   circumstance   responsible-ility

expensive

Phrases

at once   ;

82

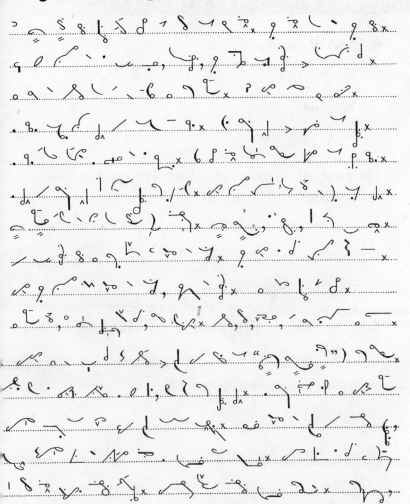

ntlemen:

The little town of Spring Lake in·this state depends upon springs and
:ams for·most of·its ground water supply. The water problem in some of·
se small towns can·be separated into several problems. These include
ply, distance, expense, the responsibility for proper use, and·fair payment.
ne home owners seem to·believe·that water and·water service should·
free of all charges and taxes. Apparently you have·found a way to·
et this difficulty that·has·been approved and accepted by·the people
your town. Won't you tell us more about your method?

Yours·very·truly,   (102)

F- and V-hooks

Finally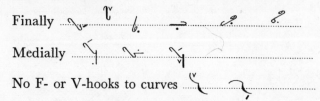

Medially

No F- or V-hooks to curves

Halving of Finally Hooked Forms for the Addition of T or D

Straight strokes with N-hook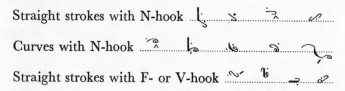

Curves with N-hook

Straight strokes with F- or V-hook

Circles and Loops Added to Hooked Strokes

Initially to R-hook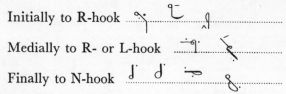

Medially to R- or L-hook

Finally to N-hook

Short Form Mastery

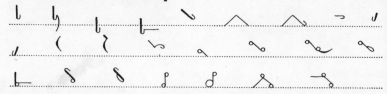

Phrase Mastery

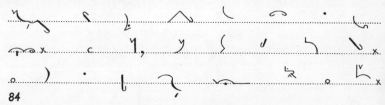

84

Letters for Dictation

A.

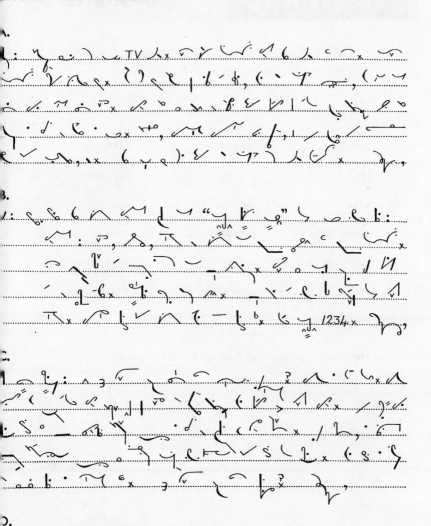

B.

C.

D.

Dear Miss Snow:

Today you·should·be·able·to take Test Four with ease and credit. Use· the same method in taking Test Four as you did with all·the others. *Think* about each outline before beginning to·write it.

head	bound	wife	dance	ground	news	often	road	towns
side	band	wave	dines	grand	nice	fan	ride	tense
reed	bind	wove	dense	grind	noise	fine	ready	tones
aid	bond	waif	dunce	grained	knows	phone	reed	tins
wood	bend	weave	deans	groaned	niece	fun	rude	tunes

Yours for·the pleasure that success brings,   *(92)*

85

Two consecutive vowel sounds pronounced separately are call
a diphone. Diphones are written as follows:

(a) ......_k_...... when the first of the two vowels is a
dot vowel.

> payable ......

payable	happier	carrying
idea	serious	appropriate
area	various	experience
radio	previous	million
premium	saying	suggestion
really	seeing	weighing
realize		

(b) ......_1_...... when the first of the two vowels is
a dash vowel.

> cooperate ......

cooperate	knowing	lower
following	showing	truer
		drawer

The first vowel of a diphone determines the place of the dipho
sign.

Short Forms

owing/language ......   together ......   altogether ......

Phrasing

In phrases, the outline for *possible* is shortened, thus:

...... ; *together with* ......

86

Reading and Writing Practice

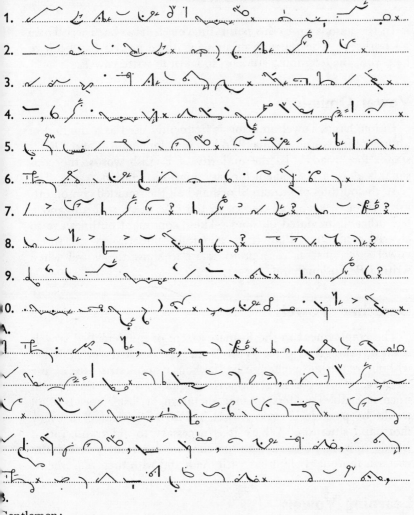

1.

2.

3.

4.

5.

6.

7.

8.

9.

10.

A.

B.

Gentlemen:

For over a year, we·have·been seriously weighing·the idea of owning our· own home. However, owing to a previous experience, we·have kept on saying "no" to each house we·have looked at. Seeing·the new homes in Rose Wood helped us to·make up our minds. We·want one of·those homes.

This·time we·want to·be certain of knowing all the details of·every amount payable. We · must know · the meaning of · the language in fine print before signing a single paper. We should like to·have your Mr. Truer meet with·us next Tuesday to explain·the various details.

Very· truly·yours,   (112)

VOWEL INDICATION

In the lessons up to this point, the vowels have been written in all outlines. The purpose of showing these vowels has been to help you, the beginning student, to learn to write vowels.

Vowel Omission

In longhand, vowel omission is frequently used as a method of abbreviating words. Thus, "Pd." stands for "paid," and "Rd." stands for "road." In the majority of English words, the consonants alone are sufficient for easy word recognition.

In the outlines of Pitman Shorthand all the sounded consonants are written—except, of course, in the case of short forms and a few other abbreviated outlines. These consonant outlines are so clearly distinctive that it is generally unnecessary to insert vowel signs, just as it is unnecessary to show the vowel when writing *Pd.* in longhand.

Detached Vowels

The employment in the Pitman system of the detached vowels is an advantageous plan. Vowels may be omitted—or added—without requiring a change in the consonantal structure of the outlines. This is a most important quality within the system since it enables writers to take dictation at faster speeds than would be possible if every vowel had to be indicated in every shorthand situation. Where it is necessary to aid transcription speed, however, vowels can quickly be inserted—*provided* the writer is thoroughly familiar with them and with their placement.

Learning Vowels

That is why the beginning student *must* learn the vowel system thoroughly. High speed writers, who omit vowels from most outlines, are the first to relate that they learned the vowels and their placings very thoroughly during the learning process so that at the advanced speed level they could insert them quickly, and insert them without conscious thought and without effort. Every experienced writer knows that it is wise to insert important vowels in unfamiliar words or unusual words, in proper names, and sometimes in one-syllable words.

Position

You know already that the first vowel in a word governs the position in which the outline is written. In transcribing, therefore, the position of an outline helps to identify the first vowel in an outline, even though the vowel sign is omitted.

Vowel Indication

In addition, the Pitman system provides a means of indicating the presence or absence of a vowel through a pattern of alternate forms. These methods of vowel indication are presented in the following four lessons (Lessons 37 to 40). Beyond this point in the text, vowels have been omitted from all outlines, except where they are beneficial for easy and rapid transcription.

Writing Vowels

When should you, the beginner, write vowels? The answer depends upon the rate of dictation. If the dictation is fast, insert necessary vowels if possible, but write consonant outlines for every word. If there is time, insert helpful vowels also. Vowels are an aid in transcription: a complete outline is read with greater speed and confidence. As a general rule, the longer the outline, the more distinctive it is, and, consequently, the less important the vowels become. But, one-syllable words, especially those with an initial vowel, are often more easily read when a vowel is inserted.

When a choice must be made between putting in vowels and getting down outlines for all of the dictation, it is better to write the outlines without vowels. Context will usually help you transcribe outlines in which consonants only are written, but nothing will help you reconstruct sentences for which you have written only half of the outlines, even though these may be complete with vowels.

The learning of the vowel signs and the learning of their placement with ease and accuracy has been an important training step towards your success as the complete and efficient high speed writer.

Now continue with your study of Pitman Shorthand, writing it as do the high speed writers around the world, making full use of the system's wonderful flexibility, readability, dependability, and speed possibilities.

(a) In order to indicate a final vowel after N, F, or V, the stroke N, F, or V is written.

penny

penny

(compare with *pen*)

many

money

(compare with *men*)

heavy

coffee

(b) In order to indicate a final vowel after T or D, the stroke T or D is written.

county

county

(compare with *count*)

sixty

honesty

(compare with *honest*)

property

safety

(compare with *sift*)

window

(compare with *wind*)

ready

body

(Note the distinguishing position for *anybody* and *nobody*.)

Short Forms

commercial-ly   executive   school

danger

Phrasing

many people   high school

Reading

In this lesson vowels are omitted from most outlines. At first this omission of vowels may cause some hesitation in reading. With practice, however, most outlines will be recognized on sight and reading speed will increase.

Remember that the position of the outline provides a clue to the first sounded vowel. Try reading the following words:

First position AH, AW, Ă, Ŏ:

Second position Ā, Ō, Ĕ, Ŭ:

Third position Ē, ŌŌ, Ĭ, ŎŌ:

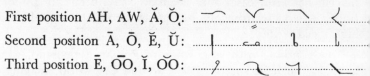

When two words can be read for an outline, choose the word that completes the sense of the sentence.

Reading and Writing Practice

1.

2.

3.

4.

5.

6.

7.

8.

9.

10.

A.

Dear Mr. Penney:

The following is a list of·the books our high-school boys have taken out most often this term: *Sixty Seconds to·Go, First Flight, Today's Men, Above· the Clouds, Honest Pen, Town and County Property, On Dangerous Sides, Safety Last, Space Travel is Ready, Cold Gold, Toward·the Skies.*

These young high-school boys seem to enjoy their visits to·the new reading classes. Already the teacher in·charge of·the extra reading classes is happy about·the boys' response. The book store costs nothing to operate commercially. The paper-covered books are cheap.

Very·truly·yours, (*101*)

91

VOWEL INDICATION: STROKES AR AND RAY

(a) When a vowel comes before R at the beginning of a word, AR is used.

early

early	arrange	art
iron	arrive	around
arm	error	ordered

(b) When a vowel follows R at the end of a word, RAY is used.

carry

carry	history	sorry
country	marry	story
factory	memory	territory
	necessary	tomorrow

Short Forms

public   publish-ed   satisfactory

Phrasing

_____ ; *let us* _____

Penmanship Improvement

Shading in itself involves no extra penmanship. The light strokes should be "hair" strokes, and there should be only the *slightest* extra pressure for the heavy strokes. All strokes should be written with a "flicking" movement. This movement can be achieved with practice, and when it has been achieved, it will be noticed that the heavy strokes taper off at the end. The slight extra pressure involved in the formation of these heavy strokes is not maintained through the writing of the stroke, but is gradually released during the writing of the stroke.

Reading and Writing Practice

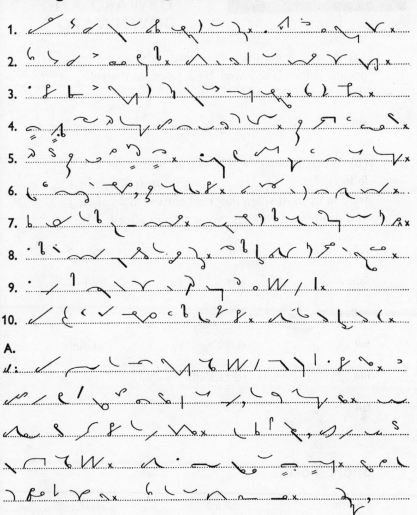

1.
2.
3.
4.
5.
6.
7.
8.
9.
10.

A.

B.

Dear Mr. Arm:

Thank·you for·the stories you have just published in·the *Iron City News*. It·is good for·the public to·have·the whole story of what has·been planned for·the factory. It·will·be necessary to·close·the plant for a time, and we· are·very·sorry that·this·is necessary. Our new machines are ordered and should arrive tomorrow. On·the earliest date we·can arrange, we·shall open again with·the largest factory in·the territory. Again may·we thank· you for carrying this story.

Yours·very·truly,   (*95*)

VOWEL INDICATION: UPWARD AND DOWNWARD L

(a) At the beginning of a word, when a vowel occurs before L followed by a horizontal stroke, downward L is used.

> alike _⟋_

alike _⟋_ _⌐_   alone _⟋_ _ſ_   along _⟋_ _⌐_

(b) When L comes at the end of an outline and follows F, V, SK, or a straight upstroke, it is written upward when the word ends with a vowel, and downward when no vowel comes after the L.

> fully _⟍_
> full _⟍_

fully _⟍_ _⟍_   fell _⟍_   rail _⟋_ _⟋_ _⟋_ _⟋_

follow _⟍_ _⟍_ _⟍_   feel _⟍_ _⟍_ _⟍_   roll _⟋_ _⟋_ _⟋_

valley _⟍_ _⟍_   fill _⟍_ _⟍_ _⟍_   rule _⟋_ _⟋_ _⟋_

fall _⟍_ _⟍_ _⟍_   skill _⟍_ _⟍_   usefully _⟍_ _⟍_

file _⟍_ _⟍_ _⟍_   successfully _⟍_ _⟍_   real _⟋_ _ſ_

fail _⟍_ _⟍_ _⟍_

Short Forms

electric _⌐_   short _⟍_ _⟍_ _ſ_   careful _⟍_ _⟍_

merely _⟍_   sure _⟍_ _⟍_   telegram _⌐_

Phrasing

_ſ_   _·⟍_   _⟍_   _⟍_

Reading and Writing Practice

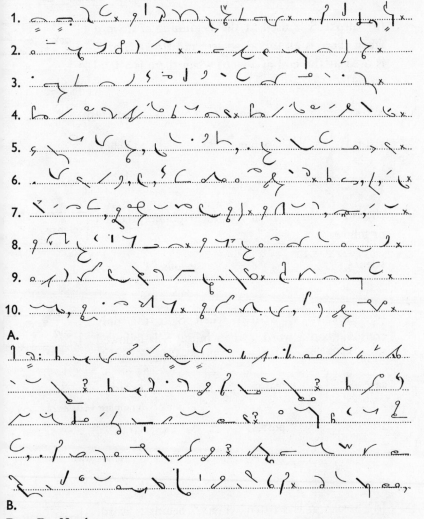

1.

2.

3.

4.

5.

6.

7.

8.

9.

10.

A.

B.

Dear Dr. North:

We·are alike in feeling that it·would·be wrong for Mr. Long to·try to· live all alone when·he goes home. It·would·be much too dangerous. If· he fell and·broke an arm or a leg, it·would surely be a very difficult thing to provide·the necessary care in·that cold little house. Perhaps a telegram to·his son in Silver Falls might have some effect.

We·are·very·sorry that·we·cannot arrange for Mr. Long's regular and satisfactory care in·his home because·of·the present Garden County rules about public·aid.

Yours·truly,   (103)

VOWEL INDICATION: STROKES S AND Z

(a) Stroke S is used at the beginning of a word when there is an initial vowel, and stroke S or Z is used at the end of a word when there is a final vowel.

ask

ask   asleep   courtesy

assist   assume   policy

busy

(b) Stroke S is written when a triphone precedes or follows S.

science

science   joyous

(c) Stroke S is written when S is the only consonant in a word; when initial S is followed by S or Z; or to obtain a distinguished outline.

saw

saw   season   excess

(compare with *cases*)

size   possess   Mrs.

(compare with *poses*)   (compare with *Misses*)

(d) Stroke Z is written when Z begins a word, or when it is the only consonant in a word.

zeal

zeal   zero   ease

Short Forms

especial-ly   establish-ed-ment

Reading and Writing Practice

1. [shorthand outlines]
2. [shorthand outlines]
3. [shorthand outlines]
4. [shorthand outlines]
5. [shorthand outlines]
6. [shorthand outlines]
7. [shorthand outlines]
8. [shorthand outlines]
9. [shorthand outlines]
10. [shorthand outlines]

A.

[shorthand outlines]

B.

Dear Jim:

When I last saw you, I said that·we hoped by means of a new advance in science to manufacture a new product. I·am now especially happy to·tell· you that·this wish has come true. Through·the zeal of·one of·our assistants we·now possess a new product that can readily be added to·our established lines. We·believe it·will easily increase our sales by many millions of dollars. We should like·you to assume charge of·the manufacture of·this new product. When can·you arrange to·come in to see me?

                    Very·truly·yours,   (*102*)

Diphones

Beginning with a dot vowel.

Beginning with a dash vowel.

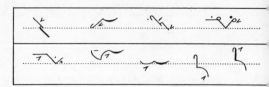

Vowel Indication

Final Vowel

    After N, F, or V

    After T or D

    After R

    After L (and F, V, SK or straight upstroke)

    After S or Z

Initial Vowel

    Before R

    Before L (and horizontal)

    Before S

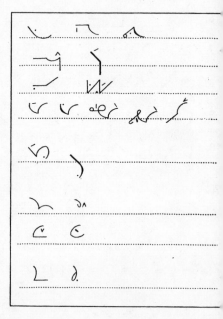

Phrasing Review

Symbol	L	P	S-circle	SEZ-circle	N-hook	F/V-hook
Written for	will	hope	us	S'S	been, than, on, own	have of
As in						

Letters for Dictation

A.

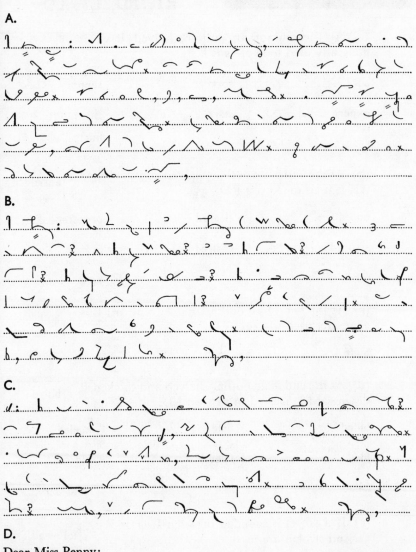

B.

C.

D.

Dear Miss Penny:

Take Test 5 in·the same manner as you did all·the others. Check each outline with·the same care.

falls	*penny*	*safety*	*windy*	*story*	*payable*	*fully*	*busy*	*asleep*
files	funny	tasty	dandy	cheery	glorious	folly	hazy	sleep
fails	sunny	hasty	candy	merry	serious	fallow	fuzzy	arrive
feels	bony	rusty	beady	curry	reality	follow	dizzy	along
fuels	skinny	dusty	Randy	Terry	heaviest	filly	lazy	long

Yours for a still better measure of·success,   (76)

(a) At the end of an outline, halved RAY is generally used to express RT.

part ....

part ....   sort ....   support ....

expert ....   start ....   But note:

report ....   hurt ....

(b) At the end of an outline, halved and thickened AR is used to express RD.

board ....

board ....   cleared ....   prepared ....

assured ....   desired ....   heard ....

card ....   hard ....

(c) At the end of an outline, halved upward L is generally used to express LT.

built ....

built ....   felt ....

(d) At the end of an outline, halved and thickened downward L is used to express LD.

billed ....

billed ....   field ....   mailed ....

filed ....   filled ....   old ....

failed ....   fold ....   child ....

(e) If a vowel is sounded between L-D or R-D, the full strokes are used.

followed ....

followed ....   valued ....   period ....

married ....

Short Forms

practice-d ....   word ....   yard ....

Reading and Writing Practice

1.

2.

3.

4.

5.

6.

7.

8.

9.

10.

A.

B.

Dear Mr. Field:

Our school is looking for a selected group of boys, between·the ages of seven and nine, with good memories. Your neighbor, Mr. Smith, has assured us that your son, John, aged nine, meets this description perfectly.

We·want to·try out a new method of language practice next term. Dr. Heard, who·is himself a language expert, is prepared to·give this special course his full support. He·has assured us of·its success with even·the youngest boys. All reports we·have received are favorable.

Would·you care to·talk to young John about joining this group?

Very·truly·yours,   (*105*)

(a) Stroke M is halved and thickened to indicate the addition of D.

made

made ....   modern ....   named ....

middle ....   seemed ....

(b) Stroke N is halved and thickened to indicate the addition of D.

end

end ....   signed ....   thousand ....

need ....   sound ....   undoubtedly ....

send ....   indicate ....

(c) Following stroke T or D, -TED is expressed by disjoined half-length T ....

credited ....   doubted ....   dated ....

Short Forms

immediate ....   individual-ly ....   prospect ....

hand ....   under ....

Intersections

Strokes may be intersected to develop short phrases.

Stroke	For	As In	
Th	month	....	several months
K	company	....	our company

Reading and Writing Practice

1. [shorthand outline]
2. [shorthand outline]
3. [shorthand outline]
4. [shorthand outline]
5. [shorthand outline]
6. [shorthand outline]
7. [shorthand outline]
8. [shorthand outline]
9. [shorthand outline]
10. [shorthand outline]

A.

[shorthand outlines]

B.

Dear Mr. Smith:

Since you·are a young married man with one child, we·think of·you as a possible home owner. We·understand you·are in·the young executive group, with every prospect of going higher. Have·you given serious thought to· the sort·of home. you want? Undoubtedly, it·is a modern home near a very·good school. We·can understand your desire to·have·the best.

We·have built several fine homes in Valley Springs which·have seemed to· meet·the immediate needs of·the young married man. Would·you care to· take a look at·them?

Very·truly·yours,   (*103*)

(a) A curve is doubled in length to indicate the addition of -TR, -DR, -THR, or -TURE.

matter

All double-length downstrokes are written through the line. When the present tense of a verb is written with a double-length stroke, the past tense is written with a halved stroke.

matter

material

motor

mother

nature

enter

center

sender

neither

another

after

further

future

father

order

(b) Where L is the only stroke, it is doubled to add TR only.

later

later

lighter

leader

But note:

letter

latter

leather

Short Forms

interest   therefore

Phrasing

I have been there ....; I know there is

Reading and Writing Practice

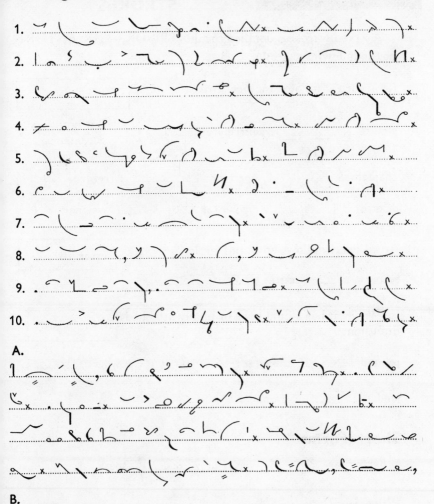

1.
2.
3.
4.
5.
6.
7.
8.
9.
10.

A.

B.

Dear Mr. Early:

Thank·you very·much for·your·letter offering to show us, free of·charge, the new materials of lighter weight now being so successfully used in clothes for growing boys. We·understand that·these materials cost less, look better, and are liked best by most boys. This·is a matter of·present and future interest to every mother of growing boys.

As every mother knows, the nature of a boy is such that·he often does·not like·the clothes his mother favors. Therefore, these new materials promise· the beginning of happier times in many families. We·feel very sure that boys' clothes of·the future are going to·please mothers and sons perfectly.

Very·truly·yours,   (*120*)

DOUBLING STRAIGHT STROKES

A straight stroke is doubled to add -TR, -DR, -THR, or -TURE in the following cases:

(a) When it follows another stroke.

picture

picture   distributor   But note: daughter

chapter   operator   reader

director   typewriter   weather

(b) When it follows an initial circle.

sector

sector   scatter

(c) When it has a final hook or finally attached diphthong.

painter

painter   winter   powder

kinder   wonder

Short Forms

rather/writer   wonderful-ly   speak

Phrasing

rather than ;   *upon their* ;   *I can be there*

Phrasing offers great speed potentialities, but it can be over-done. Some students pause to try to phrase on every possible occasion, with the result that they retard their speed. For best speed development, phrase only common word groups. Remember that a good phrase must have legibility; the words composing it must be easily joined; and it must be moderate in shorthand length.

Reading and Writing Practice

1. [shorthand outlines]
2. [shorthand outlines]
3. [shorthand outlines]
4. [shorthand outlines]
5. [shorthand outlines]
6. [shorthand outlines]
7. [shorthand outlines]
8. [shorthand outlines]
9. [shorthand outlines]
10. [shorthand outlines]

A.

[shorthand outlines]

B.

Dear Mr. Winters:

Our·company is·the biggest distributor of fine typewriters of all makes. We cover every sector of a wide territory. For·the first few days in·January of·each·year, our suppliers offer unusually high discounts. This enables us to provide even better prices.

This January, we·have allowed these wonderful values in typewriters to speak for·themselves. Do·not pass up this opportunity to·get·the new typewriters you need in·your business at·the best prices you have ever known.

Yours for better business, ‐ (89)

(a) The sounds MP and MB are expressed by the stroke .....⌢.....

> camp :⌣⌐

camp :⌣⌐

stamp ⌒

But note:

attempt .⌐⌐.

(When a consonant is only light sounded, it is omitted.)

(b) Stroke MP/MB is doubled to add R.

> December ⌐⌐⌐

December ..⌐⌐...

September .⌒⌐.

(c) The stroke NG is doubled to add GR or KR.

> longer ⌐⌐

longer .⌐⌐.

anger ⌐
anchor ⌐⌐⌐

But note: angry ⌐⌐

(d) The R-hook is also used to add KR or GR to NG and to add R to MP/MB when the resulting outline is easier to write.

> banker ⌐⌐

banker ..⌐⌐..

camper ⌐⌐

hamper ⌐⌐

stronger ⌐⌐⌐

Short Forms

important/ance ...⌐...

improve/d/ment ..⌐..

impossible ..⌐⌐..

Speed Development

Here are the 50 commonest words. Read and write the outlines until you have developed maximum speed on them.

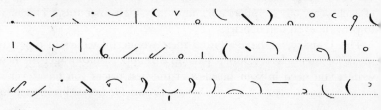

Reading and Writing Practice

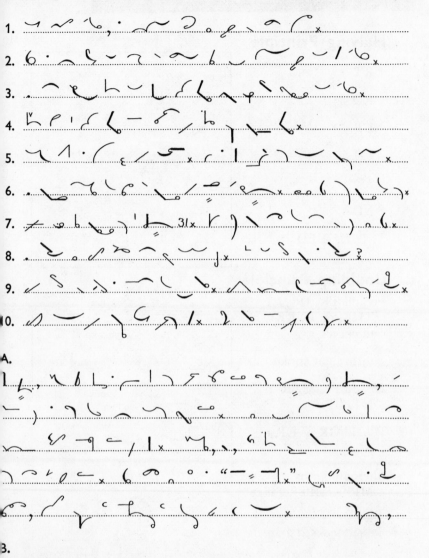

1.

2.

3.

4.

5.

6.

7.

8.

9.

10.

A.

B.

Dear Mr. Jones:

It·is time to·write you a stronger letter than we·have in·the past few·
months. Your account is no longer just due; it·is very·much past due.
Our attempts to obtain payment from·you began last September.

Please understand that·we write now not in anger, but rather with regret
that·it·is impossible for·us to·wait longer. We·are·sure you·will·understand·
the importance of sending your check immediately.

Yours·truly,   *(80)*

Halving Principle

RT

RD

LT

LD

MD

ND

-TED, -DED

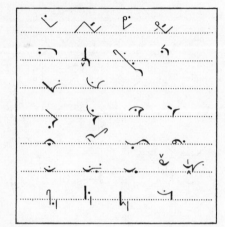

Doubling Principle

To add TR, DR, THR, or TURE to curves

to straight strokes

To add PR or BR to MP/MB

To add GR or KR to NG

Alternate forms MPPR/MPBR (after K or upstroke)

NGGR/NGKR

Non-use of doubling

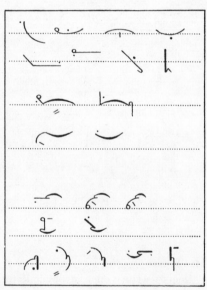

Short Form Review

(1)

(2)

Letters for Dictation

A.

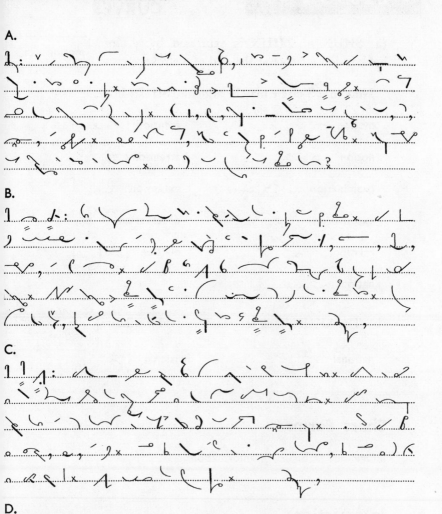

B.

C.

D.

Dear Miss System:

Today you·are going to·try your hand at Test 6.

Once more, write and check.

another	bad	billed	father	found	land	lighter	looked	stores	want
nature	bed	boiled	fighter	fond	lined	latter	liked	stars	wind
neither	obeyed	bald	feather	find	lend	loiter	lacked	stairs	went
knitter	bead	baled	feature	fund	loaned	later	locked	stirs	waned
neater	bowed	bowled	fitter	phoned	leaned	litter	leaked	steers	wound

Surely you had each word right this·time. Now you·can begin to·write faster and faster.

Yours for further shorthand success. (*91*)

SHUN-HOOK TO CURVES

(a) SHUN or ZHUN is expressed by a large hook inside a curve at the end of a stroke.

motion ....⌐....

Note that S-circle may be added to SHUN-hook.

motion ....⌐.... ....⌐.... ....⌐.... ....⌐....

mention ....⌐.... ....⌐....

notion ....⌐.... ....⌐....

attention ....⌐.... ....⌐....

examination ....⌐.... ....⌐.... ....⌐....

extension ....⌐.... ....⌐.... ....⌐....

explanation ....⌐.... ....⌐.... ....⌐....

observation ....⌐.... ....⌐.... ....⌐....

relation ....⌐.... ....⌐.... ....⌐....

division ....⌐.... ....⌐.... ....⌐....

nation ....⌐.... ....⌐....

(b) The SHUN-hook may also be used medially.

national ....⌐....

national ....⌐.... ....⌐.... ....⌐....

divisional ....⌐....

Short Forms

inform-ed ....⌐....

information ....⌐....

Intersections

Stroke	For	As In	
T	attention	your attention	....⌐....
KR	corporation	your corporation	....⌐....

Reading and Writing Practice

1.
2.
3.
4.
5.
6.
7.
8.
9.
10.
A.

Dear Mr. Masters:

As a successful engineer in·the field of modern industry, you have come to understand fully the word *responsibility* in relation to·your job. Have· you, at·the same time, applied this thought to matters relating to·your home and your family? The following information, supplied in a recent report put out by a group of nation-wide insurance·companies, may surprise and interest you. Less than half of·this country's rising young engineers are carrying enough insurance.

How·much insurance is enough? What·is your notion on·this matter?

Very·truly·yours,　　(*96*)

SHUN-HOOK TO STRAIGHT STROKES

A SHUN-hook attached to straight strokes is written:

(a) On the side opposite an initial circle or hook. | section ⌐

section ⌐   collection ⌐   station ʃ

exception ⌐   corporation ⌐

(b) On the side opposite to the last vowel if there is no initial circle or hook. | action ⌐

action ⌐   operation ⌐   perfection ⌐

caution ⌐   direction ⌐   portion ⌐

application ⌐   education ⌐   distribution ⌐

occasion ⌐

(c) On the right side of T, D, or J. | notation ⌐

notation ⌐   addition ⌐

(d) When SHUN follows the S or NS-circle, it is expressed by a small hook opposite the circle. | position ⌐

position ⌐   possession ⌐   transition ⌐

decision ⌐   taxation ⌐

Note that only third-place vowels between the S and SHUN sounds are shown. They are placed outside the hook.

(e) Endings such as *-uation* or *-uition* are expressed by the stroke SH and the N-hook. | situation ⌐

Short Forms

satisfaction ⌐   publication ⌐   organization ⌐

114

Reading and Writing Practice

1. [shorthand outline]
2. [shorthand outline]
3. [shorthand outline]
4. [shorthand outline]
5. [shorthand outline]
6. [shorthand outline]
7. [shorthand outline]
8. [shorthand outline]
9. [shorthand outline]
10. [shorthand outline]

A.

[shorthand outlines]

B.

Gentlemen:

Just send me the directions for·my part in·the clothing drive for needy children. I heard your report over·the radio on Wednesday evening and had already made my decision when your letter arrived today. My being able·to help your organization in·its efforts to assist children in need has· been the occasion of great personal satisfaction. No amount of money could provide an equal degree of satisfaction. My personal experiences in dealing with needy children have, without exception, been pleasant.

Very·truly·yours,

(87)

(a) W at the beginning of a word and followed by K, G, M, or upward or downward R is expressed by a small semicircle.

walk

walk   world   wire

wagon   worth   warm

woman   war   work

(Note position to distinguish from *women*)   were   weak/week

(b) W in the middle of a word can conveniently be expressed by a disjoined semicircle.

frequent

frequent   quality

qualify   twenty

(c) WL is expressed by

well

well   will

wall   wild

(d) WHL is expressed by

while

while

Short Forms

object-ed

Reading and Writing Practice

1.

2.

3.

4.

5.

6.

7.

8.

9.

10.

A.

B.

Dear Mr. Wild:

We·have·the wire you sent to·us today about women's walking shoes. The demand for women's walking shoes has increased very fast, and we· expect it to·go on growing for some time. Our top quality shoe sells for $15, but we also have shoes at $12 and $10. We·have a supply of all sizes in all three qualities, and·we·can deliver to·you in one week. Just tell·us what will·be needed, and·we·shall·be·glad to ship your·order without delay.

Very·truly·yours,   (94)

KWAY, GWAY, WHAY

KWAY ⌐ as in quarter	WHAY as in awhile
GWAY ⌐ as in linguist	

Outline Study

(a)

quarter

acquire

quote

quantity

quotation

square

quick

inquire

question

require

equip

request

(b) linguist

(c) awhile   where

white

Short Form

whether

Phrases

in order to ....; *very well*

Reading and Writing Practice

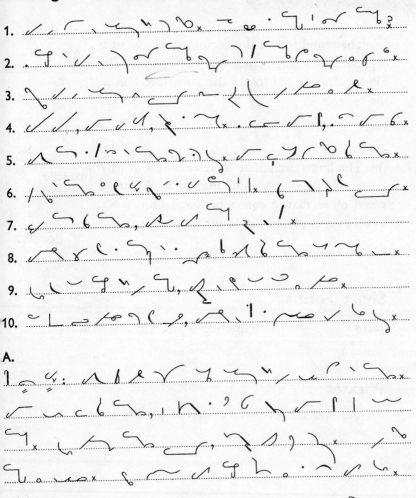

1.
2.
3.
4.
5.
6.
7.
8.
9.
10.

A.

B.

Dear Mr. Quinn:

The air force equipment you have acquired will meet our requirements very·well. We·shall need·the equipment as quickly as you·can arrange to· deliver it. Your quotation is satisfactory, and all of·our questions have·been taken care·of very·well. The enclosed order tells where each piece of equipment is·to·be delivered. Will·you let·me·know whether you·can follow these directions?

Very·truly·yours, (74)

(a) The sound SW at the beginning of a word is expressed by a large circle (called SWAY). The SWAY-circle is written in the same direction as the S-circle.

sweet	͏P

sweet .ͺP͏ ͏q ͏P........   swift .Ϙ ͏Ϙ........   swim .ͻ.ͼ: .ͻ~........

(b) The large circle that represents SES or SEZ in the middle of an outline may be used when a vowel other than ĕ comes between the two S's. The vowel is placed inside the circle.

exercise	͏ϼ

exercise ..ϼ ͏ϼ........   exhaust ..ͳ ͏ͳ........   exist ..ͳ ͳ........

Short Forms

guard ͨ..........   inspect-ed-ion ..ϗ..   thus ...(......

whose ....)......

Phrases

Note the use of SWAY in the phrases *as well as* ..ͨ..;
as we are ..ͻ..........

In phrases, *were* may be expressed by ...)...... or ..ͼ......., as in:

you were ...ͻ......; *we were* ....ͼ............

..........ͻ.................ͼ...........ϟ...........ϗ..........

Reading and Writing Practice

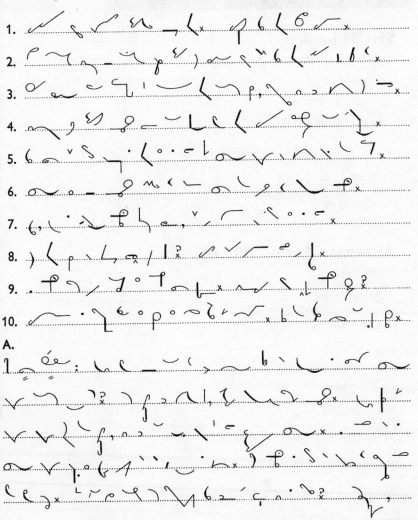

1.

2.

3.

4.

5.

6.

7.

8.

9.

10.

A.

B.

Dear Mr. Swift:

We·were told by one of·your friends that you·were interested in joining our Health Club. Let·me say that·we·have on hand equipment for every kind·of exercise. Many of·our new machines help·you to exercise so·that you do·not exhaust yourself. If·you like to swim, we·have a bright, clean pool, with a guard always on duty. We·think·you· will like our Health Club. As·we·are·now taking in members for next year, why not sign up and join·the fun?

Very·truly·yours, (96)

121

SHUN-hook

To curves
To straight strokes
    With initial attachment
    Without initial attachment
    After T, D, J
    After S or NS

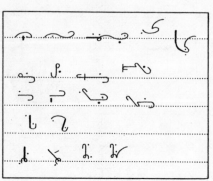

Alternate Forms for W

Semicircle
    Joined
    Disjoined

KWAY

GWAY

WL

WHL   but

WH

SWAY

SEZ Circle

    With intervening vowel

Phrase and Intersection Review

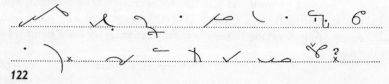

Letters for Dictation

A.

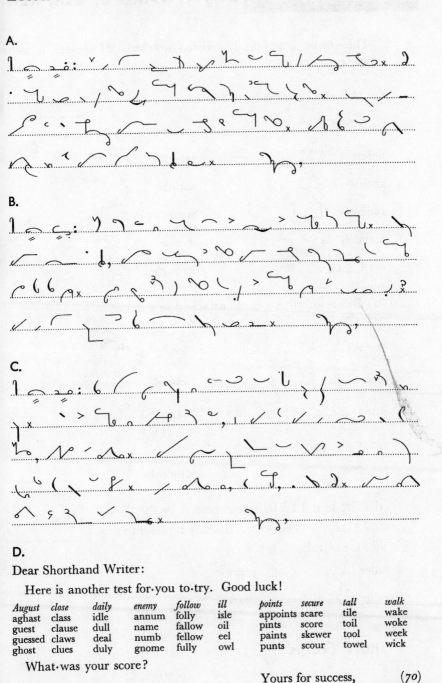

B.

C.

D.

Dear Shorthand Writer:

Here is another test for·you to·try. Good luck!

August	*close*	*daily*	*enemy*	*follow*	*ill*	*points*	*secure*	*tall*	*walk*
aghast	class	idle	annum	folly	isle	appoints	scare	tile	wake
guest	clause	dull	name	fallow	oil	pints	score	toil	woke
guessed	claws	deal	numb	fellow	eel	paints	skewer	tool	week
ghost	clues	duly	gnome	fully	owl	punts	scour	towel	wick

What·was your score?

Yours for success,   (70)

The stroke L is usually written upward. However, in some cases, L is written downward:

(a) After the strokes N and NG.

only _____ | evidently _____

unless _____ | recently _____

annual _____ | natural _____

suddenly _____ | accordingly _____

certainly _____ | increasingly _____

until _____ | strongly _____

(b) Before or after a circle attached to a curve in order to follow the direction of the circle.

vessel _____ | losing _____

lessen _____ | cancel _____

listen _____ | senseless _____

(c) For a better joining.

film _____ | additional _____

(d) The sound LER is represented by the downstroke _____. The sound RER is represented by the downstroke _____.

fuller _____ | poorer _____

ruler _____ | clearer _____

Short Forms

handle _____ | nearly _____

124

Reading and Writing Practice

1.
2.
3.
4.
5.
6.
7.
8.
9.
10.

A.

B.

Dear·Miss Nelson:

Are·you interested in saving on·your annual clothing costs? What woman is·not? Provided, of·course, that she can select hers from·the new stocks of beautiful styles every·day of·the week?

Recently a group of·our most successful buyers spent a full day at·this unusual job: "Listen to women and make careful observation of·the things they feel strongly about in·this matter of buying clothes." Naturally, our purpose was to provide in better quality and larger quantity all·the things that women want most. Visit our store to see our results.

Very·truly·yours,   (102)

(a) Stroke SH is sometimes written upwards to obtain a better outline. Generally SH follows the direction of a previous curve for a better balanced outline.

fish ....⌣....   fresh ....)....)....   dish ....

finish ....   furnish ....   appreciate....

(b) SHL is always written upward.

official ....

official

(c) SHR is always written downward.

fisher

fisher ....   fresher ....)....   pressure ....

Short Forms

sufficient-cy-ly ....   financial-ly ....

Intersections

Symbol	Stands For	As In
CH	charge	charge account ....

Useful Outlines

Practice the following outlines for the days of the week, the months of the year, and the names of the season.

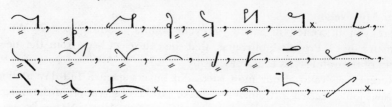

Phrases

as a matter of fact .... ; in their ....

Reading and Writing Practice

1. [shorthand outline]
2. [shorthand outline]
3. [shorthand outline]
4. [shorthand outline]
5. [shorthand outline]
6. [shorthand outline]
7. [shorthand outline]
8. [shorthand outline]
9. [shorthand outline]
10. [shorthand outline]

A.

[shorthand outlines]

B.

To·the Chairman of·the Blue Waters Fishing Club:

I should appreciate your official action on·my application to·the Blue Waters Fishing Club. I·have several friends, all fishermen, who·are club members of·long standing. On a number·of occasions recently, I·have·had· the great pleasure of going along with·them on fishing trips usually open to members only.

I appreciate that·the requirements the Blue Waters Fishing Club sets for·its members are high, but I·hope·the official action on my application will·be favorable. I·can furnish additional names for financial information.

Very·truly·yours, (101)

A. Downward R is always used before M:

room

room   firm   farm

remit   form

remain   (but notice former)

B. Upward R is used:

(a) After   sincere

answer

answer   officer

(b) After a straight upstroke.

aware

aware   refer   wiser

career   user

(c) After two straight downstrokes.

prepare

prepare   disappear   downstairs

but notice   but notice

prepared   disappeared

(d) Before

artist

artist   original   forth

arch   urge   article

storage   earth   circular

(e) To obtain a better balanced outline (especially when R follows another stroke and is hooked finally).

burn

burn   learn   portion

turn   western   prefer

Reading and Writing Practice

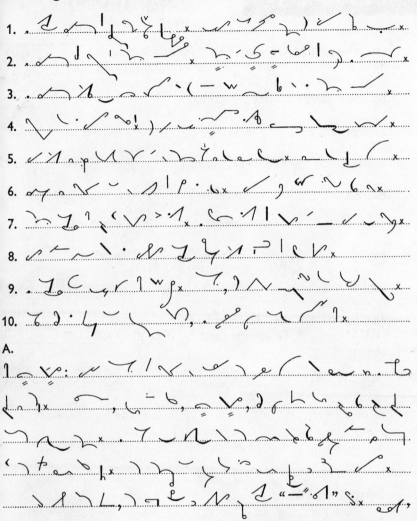

1.
2.
3.
4.
5.
6.
7.
8.
9.
10.

A.

B.

Dear Mr. Burns:

We·regret to·learn that no remittance has·been received from·you. Indeed, we·have·had no answer in reply to·our several requests. Perhaps you· are not aware that your financial standing is being affected. It·would·be wiser for·you to take care of·this matter now. We·would prefer to·have your account remain in·our hands.

We·feel sure that·you appreciate our interest, much as·we·have valued your trade in·the past. We urge you to inform us of·your present situation.

Sincerely yours, (93)

129

(a) The prefix CON-(or COM-) is expressed by a light dot placed at the beginning of the following stroke. The position of such outlines is governed by the first vowel after the prefix.

control

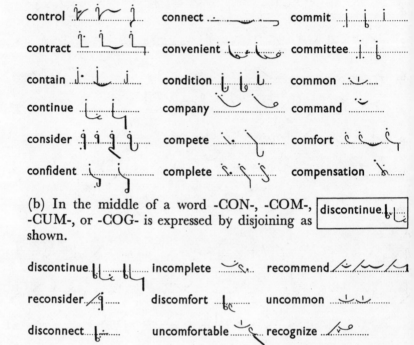

control	connect	commit
contract	convenient	committee
contain	condition	common
continue	company	command
consider	compete	comfort
confident	complete	compensation

(b) In the middle of a word -CON-, -COM-, -CUM-, or -COG- is expressed by disjoining as shown.

discontinue

discontinue	incomplete	recommend
reconsider	discomfort	uncommon
disconnect	uncomfortable	recognize

Short Forms

become   income

Phrasing

Note: *to become*

In phrasing, the prefixes CON- and COM- are indicated by writing the two outlines close together, as in *this committee*   ;
we are confident   ; *we shall continue*   ; *I will consider*

Reading and Writing Practice

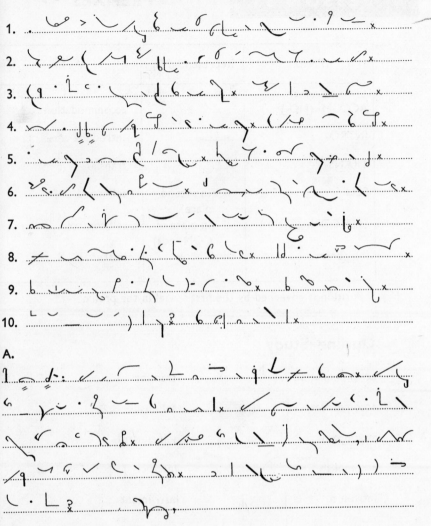

1.

2.

3.

4.

5.

6.

7.

8.

9.

10.

A.

B.

Dear Mr. Burns:

We·are in an uncomfortable situation, and·we·are asking·you to help us out·of our discomfort. We should like to discontinue something we·are doing, and·we·are·confident you·can help us. Some months ago our·company started sending·you notices of·your past due account, and·we·have·continued to·send·them to·you each·month. Would it not be·convenient for·you to complete your payments now before we turn your account over to a collection·company?

Sincerely yours,   (87)

Prefix	Represented By	As In
ACCOM- (MO-)	⎯⎯	accommodation
INTRO-	‿	introduce
TRANS-	⌐	transfer
SELF-	.o. (in second place)	self-made
SELF-CON- (COM-)	.o. (in place of CON- dot)	self-control
IN- (before figures)	small hook	instruct

Position is governed by the first vowel in the prefix.

Outline Study

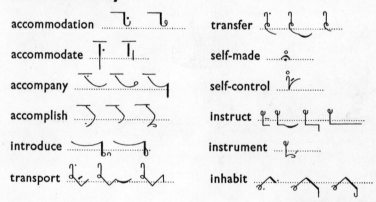

accommodation

accommodate

accompany

accomplish

introduce

transport

transfer

self-made

self-control

instruct

instrument

inhabit

Short Form

instruction

Phrases

Yours sincerely .... ; next time ....

132

Reading and Writing Practice

1. [shorthand outline]

2. [shorthand outline]

3. [shorthand outline]

4. [shorthand outline]

5. [shorthand outline]

6. [shorthand outline]

7. [shorthand outline]

8. [shorthand outline]

9. [shorthand outline]

10. [shorthand outline]

A.

[shorthand outlines]

B.

Dear Mr. White:

When·you travel, you want accommodations that·will help·you accomplish the purpose of·your trip. You want comfort so·that·you·can rest, but also you want to·be near·the center of·the city. May·we introduce you to·our hotel—one that can accommodate you properly. Our staff is instructed to help·you make your stay with·us most pleasant. Next·time you plan to visit our city, let·us show you that a transfer to·our hotel will mean much to·you.

Yours·sincerely,

(91)

133

Strokes

DOWNWARD:

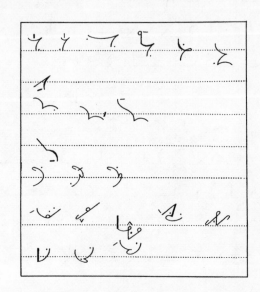

L

LER

R

RER

SH, SHR

UPWARD:
R

SH, SHL

Prefixes

Initial

CON- ⁝ ⁝ * TRANS-

COM- ⁝ ⁝ * SELF-

ACCOM-(-MO-) SELF-CON-(-COM-)

INTRO- IN- (before

)

* Position is governed by the first vowel after CON- or COM-.
In the other cases, position is governed by the first vowel in
the prefix.

Medial

-CON- -COG-

-COM- (-CUM-)

Letters for Dictation

A.

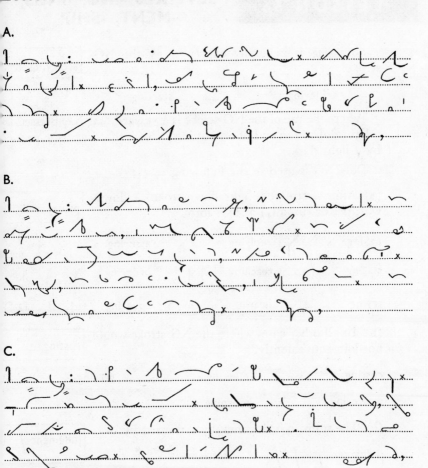

B.

C.

D.

Dear·Miss Nearly Finished:

Are·you just as interested in shorthand as you·were when·you began?
We truly hope so, and·we also hope that·these short test letters have·been
of·some assistance to·you along·the way.

annual	*lessen*	*fish*	*rush*	*room*	*answer*	*wall*	*accommodation*
only	listen	finish	push	rhyme	officer	wile	transmit
unless	loosen	vanish	blush	army	reference	well	transfer
recently	senseless	appreciate	crush	roam	roar	will	self-confident
wrongly	nasal	brush	splash	ream	circular	wool	instrument

Do·not make·the error of·lessening application now that·you·are nearing·
the finish line. This·is·the time for all-out effort.

Yours for shorthand perfection,   (*109*)

Suffix-*ing* is generally expressed by the NG-stroke.

achieving [shorthand]

achieving [shorthand]   starting [shorthand]

Where the use of the NG-stroke is awkward, -*ing* is expressed by a light dot at the end of an outline. (Note that -*ings* is expressed by a light dash.)

Dot-ING is used in the following cases:

(a) After a straight, light downstroke, a downward R, or (usually) a short form.

paying [shorthand]

paying [shorthand]   replying [shorthand]   assuring [shorthand]

stating [shorthand]   teaching [shorthand]   ordering [shorthand]

trying [shorthand]   hearing [shorthand]   covering [shorthand]

(b) In all other cases where the NG-stroke would not join conveniently.

costing [shorthand]

costing [shorthand]   meeting [shorthand]   serving [shorthand]

mastering [shorthand]   morning [shorthand]

(c) The suffix -*ment* is generally expressed by [shorthand]

judgment [shorthand]

judgment [shorthand]   settlement [shorthand]

(d) -*Ment* is sometimes expressed by [shorthand]

announcement [shorthand]

announcement [shorthand]   consignment [shorthand]

(e) The suffix -*ship* is expressed by a joined or disjoined SH.

citizenship [shorthand]

citizenship [shorthand]   friendship [shorthand]   hardship [shorthand]

Short Forms

coming [shorthand]   publishing [shorthand]   governing [shorthand]

giving [shorthand]   interesting [shorthand]   acknowledge [shorthand]

Reading and Writing Practice

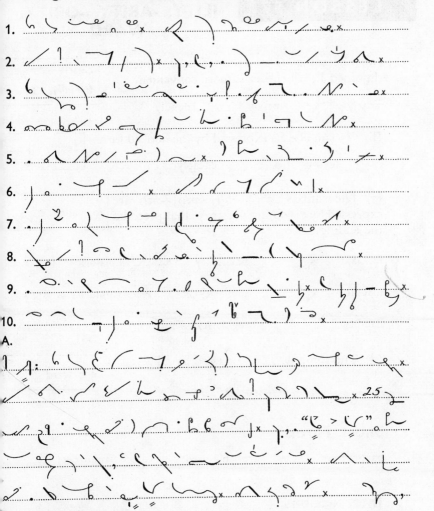

1.

2.

3.

4.

5.

6.

7.

8.

9.

10.

A.

B.

Dear·Miss Center:

Replying to·your recent letter ordering thirty yards of·covering materials for·your new custom-made chairs, we·regret very·much indeed that·we·are· unable·to serve you at·this·time. Because of high costs and·the difficulty of obtaining these unusual materials, we·are·obliged to·limit their sale.

Our announcement stating the terms of·this special sale of unusual chair covering materials was mailed to·our charge·customers over two·months ago. In·order·to get·the materials we·wanted at·such favorable prices, we ourselves had to·make full payment in·advance.

Very·truly·yours,   (102)

SUFFIXES -LY, -ALITY, -ILITY, -ARITY, -ORITY, -WARD

(a) The suffix -*ly* is expressed by a joined or disjoined L, whichever is more convenient.

| clearly |
| friendly |

clearly   mainly   friendly

(b) -*Ly* can also be expressed by the hooked form.

| deeply |

deeply   cheaply

(c) The suffixes -*ality*, -*ility*, -*arity*, -*ority* are expressed by disjoining the stroke that precedes the ending.

| formality |

formality   possibility   majority

inability   similarity   minority

liability   regularity

(d) The suffix -*ward* is expressed by a halved W.

| forward |

forward

Short Forms

particularly   probable-ly-ility   familiar-ity

Intersections

Stroke	For	As In
D	department	billing department
M	morning	this morning

When a stroke cannot be conveniently intersected, it may be written close to the preceding stroke; as in, *credit department* ; *new company*

Dear·Miss Mills:

Possibly you have already heard something about·the modern, and wonderfully·convenient way to assure your taking·the trip to·which·you have·been looking forward these many·years. Probably more people have·taken advantage of·the World Airlines plan to "Go now and pay later" this summer than ever before. Have·you·considered it at·all, Miss Mills? Everybody likes to travel and to see far places. Our records for·the·months of·June, July, and August, indicate a particularly high percentage of "pay-later" trips. May·we·have our credit·department send·you full details?

Very·truly·yours,   (*103*)

Suffix	Represented By	As In
-MENTAL-LY	⌒ ⎫	fundamental-ly ⌒⌒
-FULNESS	⌒ ⎬ disjoined	hopefulness ⌒
-LESSNESS	⌒ ⎪	hopelessness ⌒
-LOGICAL-LY	/ ⎭	psychological-ly /
-YARD	⌒ joined	back yard ⌒

Outline Study

fundamental-ly ⌒⌒   psychological-ly /

hopefulness ⌒   back yard ⌒

hopelessness ⌒

Short Forms

carefulness ⌒   carelessness ⌒

Review

See how many times in a minute you can write the following outlines: they represent words which you will be called upon to write many times in the course of your shorthand career:

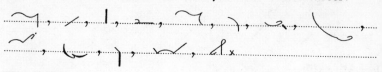

Phrasing

Note how *afternoon* and *evening* can be represented in phrases:

Friday evening ⌒, *Monday afternoon* ⌒

Now practice these outlines:

Reading and Writing Practice

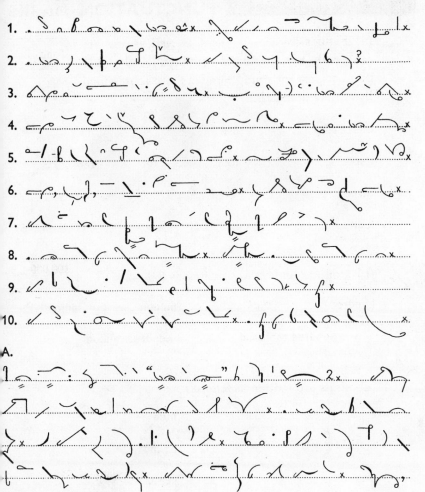

1.

2.

3.

4.

5.

6.

7.

8.

9.

10.

A.

B.

Dear Dr. Wise:

As a committee member·of·the recently formed Western College Readers Club, I·have·been requested to·write you asking whether·you would·be willing to·speak at our December meeting. The club has selected psychology as·its first reading project. Among·the books already read in·connection with·this special field are three of·yours. They·are *Fundamentals of Psychology*, *The Psychology of Learning*, and *Psychology in Daily Living*. These three have served a very useful purpose. We quickly discovered·the truth of·the well·known quotation, "A little learning is a dangerous thing."

Yours·very·truly,   (*101*)

(a) Figures from *one* to *seven* as well as *nine* are expressed by shorthand outlines. All other numbers, except round numbers, are represented by Arabic numerals.

one	⟋

one	⟋	five	⟍	nine	⌣
two	⟍	six	⟀	ten	⌡
three	⟩	seven	ℓ	twenty	⌐
four	⟍	eight	8	fifty-seven	57

(b) Round numbers are written as follows:

300,000	3

hundred ⌣   thousand ⟨   million ⌢   billion ⟍

hundred thousand ⟋   hundred million ⌢

(c) Units are written as follows:

cent ⟀ ⟀   mile ⟋ ⟋ ⟋

dollar | ƅ   pound ⟋ ⟍

inch ⟋ ⟋   per cent ⟍ ⟍

(d) Figures and units are combined as follows:

6,000 pounds	6ƅ

6,000 pounds ...6ƅ... $10,000 ...10ƅ...

(e) Punctuation marks are written as follows:

Period ...×...   Exclamation ..!×..   Dash ⟋

Question ..?×..   Hyphen ..=..   Parentheses ( )

Reading and Writing Practice

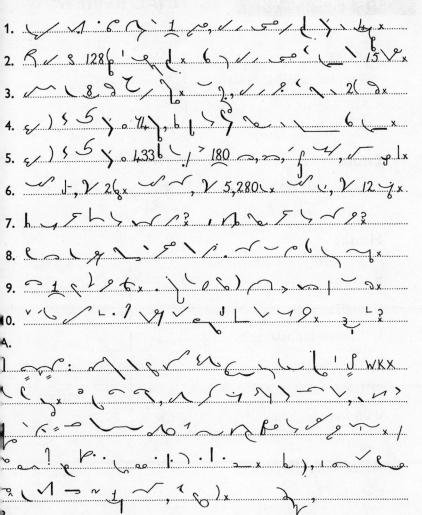

1.

2.

3.

4.

5.

6.

7.

8.

9.

10.

A.

B.

Dear Mr. Pound:

Would·you·be willing to answer a fair question—at·least, we·consider it
fair! Why is·it that·we·cannot save a cent, no matter how hard we try?
Our family income is ten·thousand·dollars a year. We·have two young
children, a boy ten years old and a girl of six.

We·have·been following your articles in·the evening section of THE
WORLD for·several·months. Everybody else in·our circumstances seems to·
have an extra thousand or two·thousand·dollars at·the·end of·the·year. What·
is·the matter with·us? How·can·we save?

Very·truly·yours,   (107)

143

FINAL REVIEW

Circles

S (initial, medial, final)

SW (initial)

SEZ (medial, final)

Loops

ST (initial, medial, final)

STER (medial, final)

Hooks

TO STRAIGHT STROKES	TO CURVES
R (initial, medial)	
L (initial, medial)	
F/V (medial, final)	
N (medial, final)	
SHUN (medial, final)	
With S-circle (initial, medial, final)	

Alternate Forms

L

R

S, Z

SH

H

W, WH

FR, VR, THR

FL, VL

Reading and Writing Practice

1.
2.
3.
4.
5.
6.
7.
8.
9.
10.

A.

B.

Dear Mr. Wall:

　We·take·pleasure in·informing you that·you·are one·of·the winners who· will receive·the daily and Sunday editions of·the *Record* free for four years. Your name was selected from a list of· promising young· men who spent· the past summer working in different parts of· the· country gathering· the materials that· make· the news. You·were selected by experienced judges who considered·the worth of·the individual reports.

　We·are·very happy to open·the door of opportunity to·those·who·are now on·their way up.

Very·truly·yours,　　(97)

Suffixes

-ING: Stroke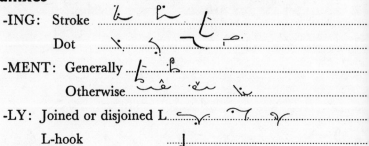

Dot

-MENT: Generally

Otherwise

-LY: Joined or disjoined L

L-hook

Notice that the choice of form is usually determined by the ease of joining.

-ALITY, -ILITY   -WARD

-ARITY, -ORITY   -YARD

-MENTAL-LY

-FULNESS

-LESSNESS

-LOGICAL-LY

-SHIP

Notice the disjoining of the final stroke to indicate the addition of a suffix.

Figures

8   1 2 3

Units

5   15   57

Intersection Review

Letters for Dictation

A.

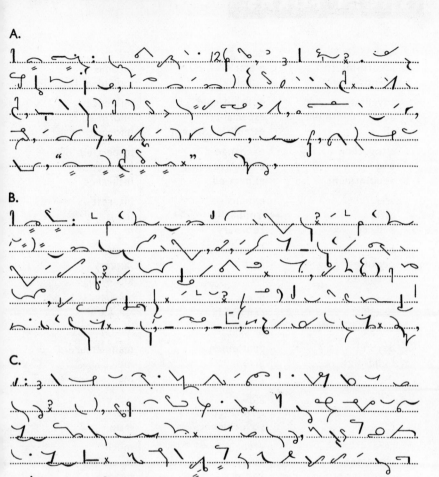

B.

C.

D.

Dear Miss Shorthand Writer:

   Today you·will·be trying to beat your·own best record by getting a perfect mark and finishing faster than you ever have before. Follow·the directions already given, then check and·practice.

air	chase	earth	force	freight	happy	land	mailed	size	wire
ire	choice	wrath	affairs	fright	hop	lend	mild	sauce	war
ore	chess	wraith	farce	fraught	hope	lined	mauled	says	were
area	cheese	wreath	furs	fret	heap	loaned	mold	seize	wear
era	choose	Ruth	fierce	fruit	hoop	leaned	milled	sues	wore

Did you make it without hesitating on a single outline?

Yours with very best wishes,   (106)

147

SHORT FORMS

a/an
accord-ing/to
acknowledge

advantage
advertise-d-ment
all

altogether
and
appointment

are
as/has
balance

be
because
become

been
behalf
belief/ve-ved

beyond
build-ing
but

call
can
cannot

care
character
characteristic

circumstance
come
commercial-ly

could
danger
dear

deliver-ed-y
description
different-ce

difficult
do
doctor/Dr.

during
electric
equal-ly

equaled/cold
especial-ly
establish-ed-ment

exchange-d
executive
expect-ed

expensive
familiar-ity
February

financial-ly
first
for

from
general-ly
gentleman

gentlemen
give-n
go

gold
govern-ed
government

great
guard
had/dollar

hand
have
he

him
himself
how

however
I/eye
immediate

important-ce
impossible
improve-d-ment

in/any
income
individual-ly

influence
inform-ed
information

inspect-ed-ion
instruction
insurance

interest
is/his
it

itself
January
knowledge

language/owing
large
liberty

manufacture-d
me
member/remember-ed

mere/Mr.
more/remark-ed
most

much
myself
near

never/November
next
nor

number-ed
object-ed
of

on
opinion
opportunity

organization
organize-d
ought

148

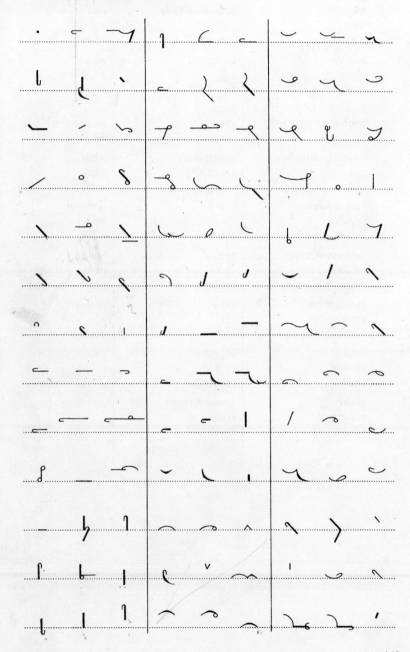

our/hour
ourselves
over

owe/oh
own
particular

people
pleasure
practice-d

principal-ly/principle
probable-ly-ility
prospect

public/publish-ed
put
quite

rather/writer
regular
represent-ed

representative
respect-ed
responsible-ility

satisfaction
satisfactory
school

sent
several
shall

short
should
speak

special-ly
spirit
subject-ed

sufficient-cy-ly
sure
surprise

telegram
tell
thank-ed

that
the
them

themselves
there/their
therefore

thing
think
third

this
those
though

thus
till
to

together
told
too/two

toward/trade
tried
truth

under
usual-ly
very

was
we
what

when
whether
which

who
whose
why

wish
with
within

without
wonderful-ly
word

would
yard
year

yesterday
you
young

your

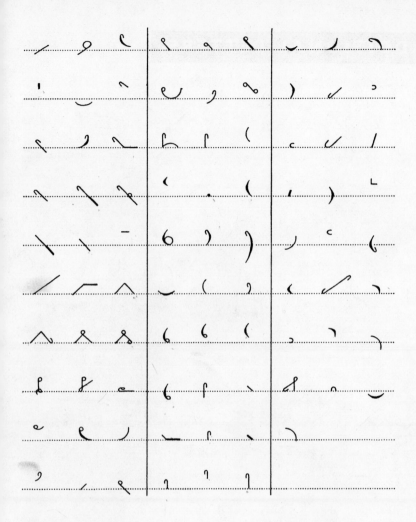

151

1

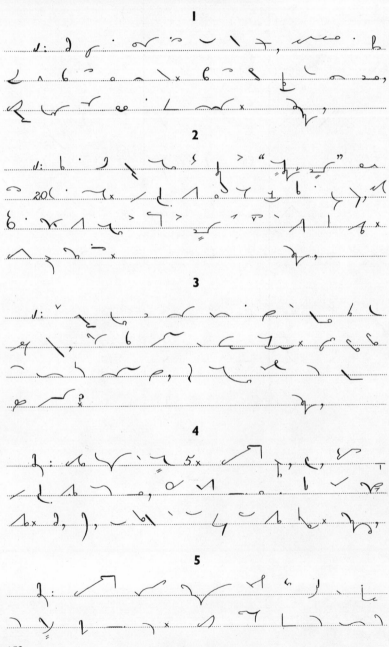

2

3

4

5

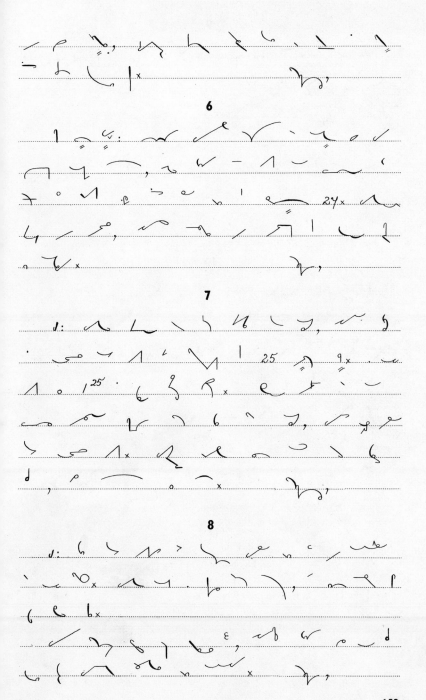

6

7

8

9

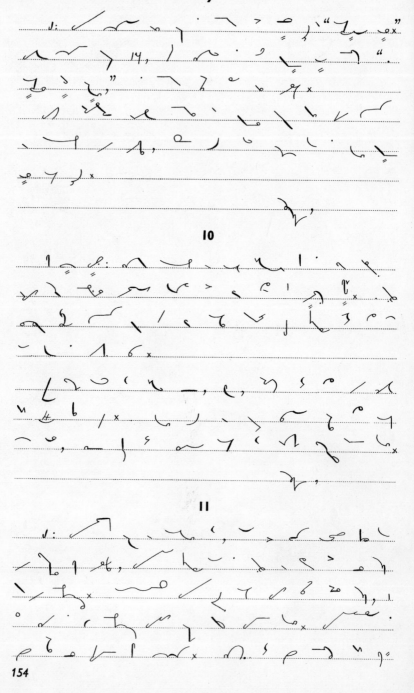

10

11

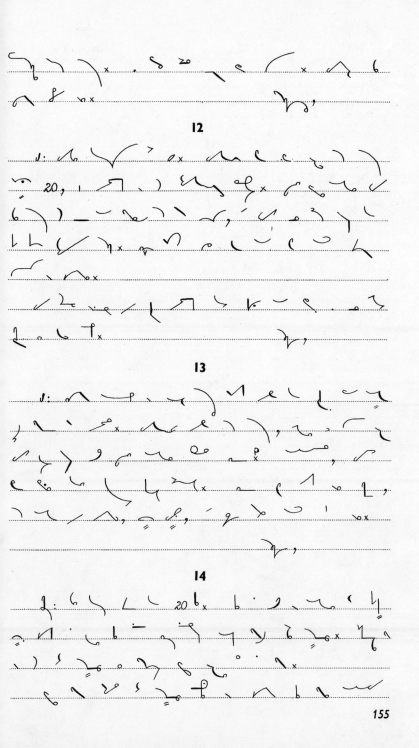

12

13

14

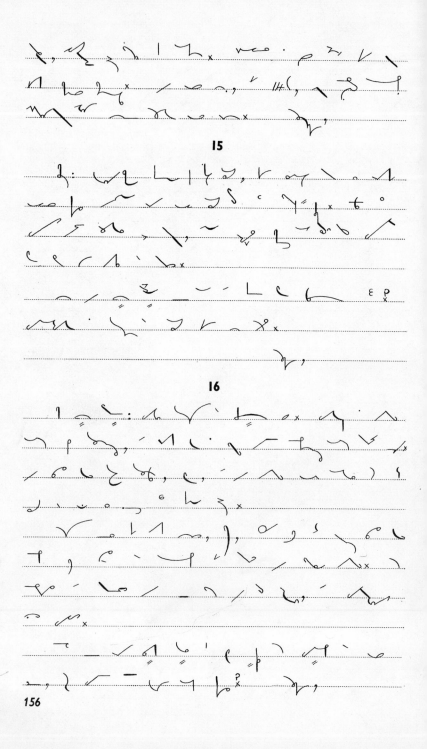

15

16

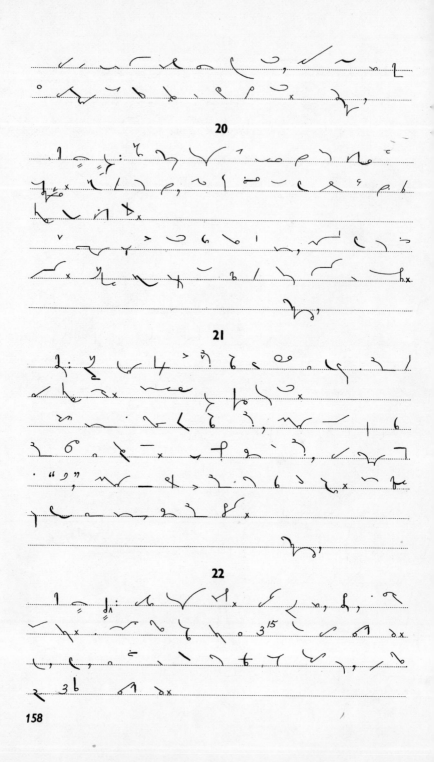

20

21

22

23

24

25

50

40

26

27

28

29

30

31

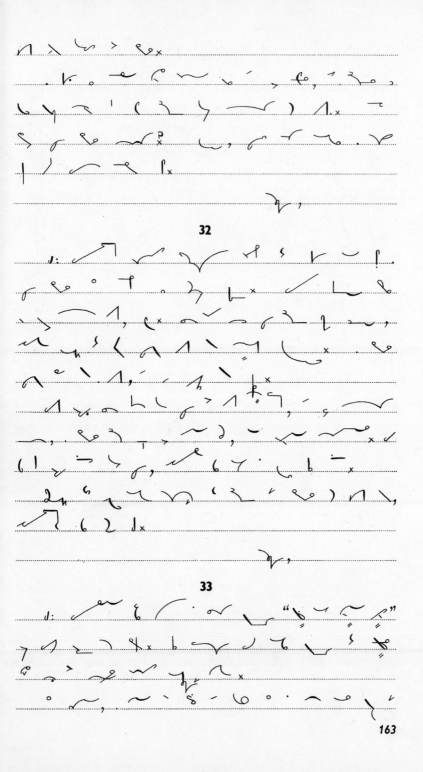

32

33

34

35

36

37

38

39

40

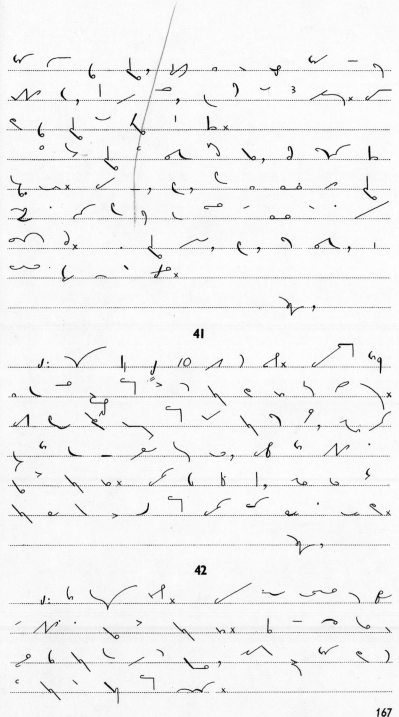

41

42

43

44

45

46

47

48

49

50

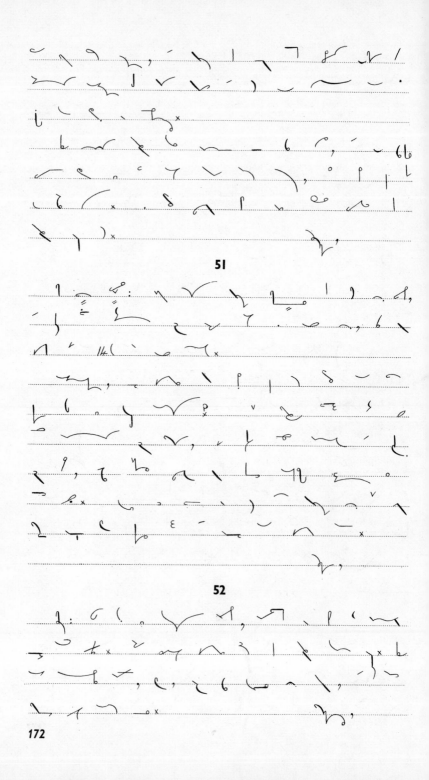

51

52

53

54

55

56

57

58

59

60